SECOND EDITION

QuickBooks® ONLINE

FOR ACCOUNTING

Glenn Owen

 CENGAGE

Australia • Brazil • Mexico • Singapore • United Kingdom • United States

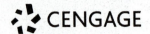

***QuickBooks® Online For Accounting,
Second Edition***
Glenn Owen

Vice President, General Manager, Social Science & Qualitative Business: Erin Joyner

Product Director: Jason Fremder

Product Manager: Christopher Rader

Project Manager: Julie Dierig

Content Developer: Erica Longenbach

Product Assistant: Aiyana Moore

Marketing Manager: Emily McClellan

Manufacturing Planner: Doug Wilke

Intellectual Property Analyst: Brittani Morgan

Cover Image Credit: ©blinkblink/Shutterstock

Art and Cover Direction, Production Management, and Composition:
Lumina Datamatics, Inc.

For product information and technology assistance, contact us at
Cengage Learning Customer & Sales Support, 1-800-354-9706.

For permission to use material from this text or product, submit all requests online at **www.cengage.com/permissions.**
Further permissions questions can be emailed to
permissionrequest@cengage.com.

Library of Congress Control Number: 2017936129

ISBN: 978-1-337-39987-6

Cengage Learning
20 Channel Street
Boston, MA 02210
USA

Cengage Learning is a leading provider of customized learning solutions with employees residing in nearly 40 different countries and sales in more than 125 countries around the world. Find your local representative at:
www.cengage.com.

Cengage Learning products are represented in Canada by
Nelson Education, Ltd.

For your course and learning solutions, visit **www.cengage.com.**

Purchase any of our products at your local college store or at our preferred online store **www.cengagebrain.com.**

Printed in the United States of America
Print Number: 04   Print Year: 2018

Brief Contents

Chapter 1   An Introduction to QuickBooks Online Plus   1

Chapter 2   Sample Company Walkthrough   15

Chapter 3   Setting Up a New Company   34

Chapter 4   Operating Activities: Sales and
            Cash Receipts   58

Chapter 5   Operating Activities: Purchases
            and Cash Payments   78

Chapter 6   Investing and Financing Activities   102

Chapter 7   Payroll   118

Chapter 8   Budgets and Bank Reconciliations   137

Chapter 9   Adjusting Entries   156

Chapter 10 Financial Statements and Reports   171

Appendix   192

Index   194

Contents

Preface   vi

About the Author & Dedication   ix

Note to the Student
and Instructor   x

Chapter 1 An Introduction to QuickBooks Online Plus   1

Overview   1
What Is QBO?   1
How Is QBO Similar/Different than the
    Desktop Version QuickBooks?   2
Creating a New QBO Account   3
Providing QBO Information   4
Navigating QBO   6
Assigning an Instructor as the
    Company's "Accountant"   10
Using QBO's Help Feature   11
End Note   13
Chapter 1 Practice   14
Chapter 1 Questions   14
Chapter 1 Matching   14

Chapter 2 Sample Company Walkthrough   15

Overview   15
Begin Your Sample Company Walkthrough   15
Customers, Vendors, and Employees   16
Banking Transactions   21
Sales and Expense Transactions   23
Chart of Accounts   25
Lists   27
Reports   28
Company Settings   31
End Note   32
Chapter 2 Practice   33
Chapter 2 Questions   33
Chapter 2 Matching   33

Chapter 3 Setting Up a New Company   34

Overview   34
Company Settings   35

Modify the Chart of Accounts and
    Establish Beginning Balances   36
Close Opening Balance Equity and
    Create a Balance Sheet   43
Create, Print, and Export a Transaction
    Detail by Account   45
End Note   47
Chapter 3 Practice   48
Chapter 3 Questions   48
Chapter 3 Matching   48
Chapter 3 Cases   48
Case 1   49
Case 2   52
Case 3   54

Chapter 4 Operating Activities: Sales and Cash Receipts   58

Overview   58
Services, Products, and Customers   58
Sales Receipts and Invoices   62
Cash Receipts   65
Transaction Detail by Account   68
End Note   69
Chapter 4 Practice   70
Chapter 4 Questions   70
Chapter 4 Matching   70
Chapter 4 Cases   70
Case 1   71
Case 2   73
Case 3   75

Chapter 5 Operating Activities: Purchases and Cash Payments   78

Overview   78
Vendors   78
Purchase Orders   79
Bills   82
Payment of Bills, Use of a Credit Card,
    Payments for Items Other than Bills   86
Trial Balance   89
End Note   92
Chapter 5 Practice   93
Chapter 5 Questions   93

Chapter 5 Matching	93
Chapter 5 Cases	93
Case 1	94
Case 2	96
Case 3	98

Chapter 6 Investing and Financing Activities **102**

Overview	102
Fixed Assets	102
Long-Term Investments	105
Common Stock and Dividends	106
Long-Term Debt	107
Acquisition of a Fixed Asset in Exchange for Long-Term Debt	109
End Note	110
Chapter 6 Practice	111
Chapter 6 Questions	111
Chapter 6 Matching	111
Chapter 6 Cases	111
Case 1	112
Case 2	113
Case 3	115

Chapter 7 Payroll **118**

Overview	118
Employees	118
Payroll Accounts	120
Pay Employees	121
End Note	127
Chapter 7 Practice	128
Chapter 7 Questions	128
Chapter 7 Matching	128
Chapter 7 Cases	128
Case 1	129
Case 2	131
Case 3	134

Chapter 8 Budgets and Bank Reconciliations **137**

Overview	137
Budget Creation	137
Budget Reports	140
Bank Reconciliation	144
End Note	148
Chapter 8 Practice	149
Chapter 8 Questions	149

Chapter 8 Matching	149
Chapter 8 Cases	149
Case 1	150
Case 2	152
Case 3	154

Chapter 9 Adjusting Entries **156**

Overview	156
Trial Balance	157
Adjusting Journal Entries: Prepaid Expenses	158
Adjusting Journal Entries: Accrued Expenses	161
Adjusting Journal Entries: Unearned Revenue	162
Adjusting Journal Entries: Accruing Revenue	163
Adjusting Journal Entries: Depreciation	164
End Note	166
Chapter 9 Practice	167
Chapter 9 Questions	167
Chapter 9 Matching	167
Chapter 9 Cases	167
Case 1	168
Case 2	168
Case 3	169

Chapter 10 Financial Statements and Reports **171**

Overview	171
Income Statement	172
Balance Sheet	174
Statement of Cash Flows	177
Accounts Receivable Aging Summary	179
Accounts Payable Aging Summary	181
Inventory Valuation Summary	183
Customizing and Saving Reports	185
End Note	187
Chapter 10 Practice	188
Chapter 10 Questions	188
Chapter 10 Matching	188
Chapter 10 Cases	188
Case 1	189
Case 2	190
Case 3	190

Appendix	**192**
Index	**194**

Overview

Accounting has arrived in the Cloud and its time has come. *Cloud computing* is a general term for anything that involves delivering hosted services over the Internet. According to a recent study by KPMG (a global network of professional firms), businesses large, medium, and small are using the Cloud to drive cost efficiencies, better enable a mobile workforce, and improve alignment with their customers and vendors.

Imagine being able to update your business's accounting information system from anywhere on any device using any operating system. That is where the global economy is going. Are you on the path?

Is This Text for You?

This text is for you if you are an instructor who desires a self-paced, self-directed environment for your students to learn the essentials of QuickBooks Online Plus (QBO) and to review their understanding of financial accounting and reporting.

This text is for you if you are a business owner looking for a self-paced, self-directed environment for yourself to learn the essentials of QBO as well as a means to refresh your understanding of financial accounting and reporting.

This book focuses on QBO. It is not designed for users of QuickBooks Pro, Accountant, or any other desktop version of QuickBooks. In that case, my QuickBooks Accountant books are a better fit. The desktop version and online versions are different, and though you can import files created in the desktop version into the online version, significant differences exist as discussed in Chapter 1.

Instructional Design

Each chapter of this text begins with a listing of expected student learning outcomes followed by a step-by-step explanation of how to obtain those outcomes. In most chapters, the explanations utilize a Sample Company created by Intuit in which the author demonstrates how various operating, investing, and financing activities of a business are captured and then reported in QBO.

End of chapter questions, matching, and three student cases follow these explanations. The questions help you to review the text-explained concepts and processes, while the matching section helps with terms and definitions. The student cases provide the information necessary to add data to the student's company file. Each chapter requires the student to add information to the previous chapter's rendition. Thus, for success in learning, each student must complete the previous chapter's student case before attempting the next chapter's student case.

Each copy (license) of QBO will work with one and only one company other than the sample company provided online. In the author's other QuickBooks texts, multiple cases were available for illustration and practice. However, because of Intuit's limit of one company per license, that option was absent unless the user purchased multiple licenses, which was impractical and costly.

Solutions to each chapter's student case are provided in the instructor manual.

Comprehensive Problems

Additional transactions for cases 1, 2, and 3 can be found on the Instructor's Companion site at Cengage. Students who have successfully completed a case in the text through Chapter 10 can be assigned these comprehensive problems. Each pick up in the month following the chapter work. For example in case 1, chapter work occurred in January 2018, thus the comprehensive problem will describe transactions occurring in February 2018. The transactions included in February are similar in nature to those described in chapters 3 through 10. Students assigned case 1 would be able to complete comprehensive case 1. Those assigned case 2 would only be able to complete comprehensive case 2 etc.

Textbook Goals

This textbook takes a user and a preparer perspective by illustrating how accounting information is created and then used for making decisions. QBO is user-friendly and provides point-can-click simplicity and sophisticated accounting reporting and analysis tools. The textbook uses proven and successful instructional design (described earlier) to demonstrate the application's features and elicit student interaction.

The first and foremost goal of this text is to help students review fundamental accounting concepts and principles through the use of the QBO application and the analysis of business events. The content of this text complements the first course in accounting principles or financial accounting. Thus this text should either be used concurrently with an accounting principles or financial accounting course or be used subsequent to completion of such a course.

A second goal of this text is to teach students how to set up QBO for a business, use it to record business events, and use it to generate financial statements and reports. Acquiring these skills will help students improve their job prospects whether the company they work for uses QuickBooks or not.

A third goal of this text is to teach students the value of a computerized accounting information system and how it can be used to communicate important information to business owners, investors, and creditors.

Date Warning

The Sample Company (created and maintained by Intuit) is used to demonstrate many aspects of QBO in this text. The author has no control over the dates used by Intuit and those dates may change depending on when you are accessing the file online. The dates that appear in the figures supplied by the author in this text may not be the dates that appear on your screen.

The student cases are set in 2018, 2019, and 2020. If transactions are entered into the student case in other than the proper period, answers will be wrong. Be careful about entering dates into QBO when you are working on this case. The default date when entering new transactions into QBO is the computer's system date that may or may not be in 2018, 2019, or 2020.

Update Warning

QBO is frequently upgraded by Intuit to provide new features, correct errors, or improve functionality. This book was written in late 2016 and early 2017 and all figures are based on how QBO looked at that time. If you are using this text in 2017 or later, Intuit may have made modifications in how QBO looks and feels or functions. Differences will occur, which are out of the author's control.

Instructor as Your Accountant

Your instructor may choose to have you assign him or her as your accountant so he or she can see your work and progress at his or her convenience without having you to "send" the file. In fact, you cannot "send" your file since all the files are on the Cloud. Instructions on how to set your instructor as your accountant are provided in Chapter 1.

Video Demonstrations

Video demonstrations, created in 2015 and updated in 2017, are available throughout this text and are referenced by a Demonstration Icon in the margin. These demonstrations are stand-alone full-action videos with audio showing step-by-step illustrations of business processes explained in this text. Intuit may have made some changes in how QuickBooks Online looks and functions, which may not be reflected in these videos. However, the author believes the videos in their present form convey the important steps and functions and are beneficial to students.

All of these are available via the text's companion website located at http://www.cengagebrain.com. Navigate your browser to http://www.cengagebrain.com. Type Glenn Owen in the Search for Books or Materials text box, and then click Find. Locate and then click the QuickBooks Online text from the listing provided.

Click the Free Materials tab and then click Access Now. When you navigate your browser to the student companion site for the text, you should see Video Demonstrations. Video Demonstrations need to be downloaded from the companion site to your computer by clicking the Video Demonstrations text. Usually these files are downloaded to a folder on your computer called Downloads. In some cases you may be asked where you want these files downloaded.

The file you download is a very large compressed zip file. When you double click the file downloaded, you'll see a list of files. All of these need to be extracted (decompressed) first before you can view them. Click Extract to a folder, and then create a folder on your computer or flash drive that you want to contain all of your demonstration files. Remember where you extracted these files so you can find them later.

About the Author

Glenn Owen is a retired member of Allan Hancock College's Accounting and Business faculty, where he lectured on accounting and information systems from 1995 to 2016. In addition, he is a retired lecturer at the University of California at Santa Barbara, where he taught accounting and information systems courses from 1980 to 2011. His professional experience includes five years at Deloitte & Touche as well as vice president of finance positions at Westpac Resources, Inc., and Expertelligence, Inc. Mr. Owen completed his 4th edition of his Using Excel and Access in Accounting text in 2016, which gives accounting students specific, self-paced instruction on the use of spreadsheets (Excel 2016) and database applications (Access 2016) in accounting. He has also recently completed the 14th edition of his QuickBooks Accountant for Accounting 2015 text, which is also a self-paced, case-based instruction on the use of a commercial accounting application (QuickBooks 2015). QuickBooks 2015 is the most recent version of the desktop product available for educational labs even though they continue to produce a commercial desktop product. His innovative teaching style emphasizes the decision maker's perspective and encourages students to think creatively. His graduate studies in educational psychology and his 41 years of business experience yield a balanced blend of theory and practice. Mr. Owen was presented the Lifetime Achievement Award in August 2016 by the Two-Year section of the American Accounting Association.

Dedication

I would like to thank my wife Kelly for her support and assistance during the creation of this and previous editions of this text. Though our boys are out of the house and pursuing their own interests, she continues to listen to my often crazy ideas for new cases and experiences with college students, providing an excellent sounding board and reality check. You and the boys continue to define what life is all about.

Note to the Student and Instructor

The text and related data files created for this book were constructed using QuickBooks Online. In this version of QuickBooks, Intuit continues its use of a basic payroll service but has made it more accessible by having it live on its Cloud-based system. QuickBooks Online initially comes with the current tax tables; however, these tables soon become outdated, and the payroll feature is disabled unless the user subscribes to the payroll service.

The author decided to use the manual payroll tax feature, which requires that students manually enter the tax deductions. This alleviates the discrepancies between the solutions manual and the students' data entry and removes the burden of having to purchase the tax table service for each copy of QuickBooks Online used. Instructions on how to set up payroll for manual calculation of payroll taxes are provided in the text. For more information, see your QuickBooks Online documentation.

All reports have a default feature that identifies the basis in which the report was created (e.g., accrual or cash) and the date and time the report was printed. The date and time shown on your report will, of course, be different from that shown in this text.

An Introduction to QuickBooks Online Plus

Student Learning Outcomes

Upon completion of this chapter, the students will be able to do the following:

- Identify the basic features of QuickBooks Online Plus (QBO)
- Explain how QBO is similar and differs from the desktop version of QuickBooks
- Create a new QBO account using codes provided with this text
- Provide information to QBO about your company
- Successfully navigate the QBO home page
- Assign their instructor as their "Accountant"
- Use QBO's help feature

Overview

The focus of this chapter is to introduce you to QuickBooks Online Plus (QBO) and get your account and company established. A description of QBO will be provided along with a brief comparison of how QBO differs from its desktop version. This text includes codes, which will allow you to create your own personal account with Intuit and create one and only one company. You will assign your company a name that includes your name for identification purposes. Welcome to the journey.

What Is QBO?

QBO is an online version of the popular QuickBooks accounting software developed by Intuit. The software is designed to capture common business events like purchases from and payments to vendors, sales to and collections from customers, payments and receipts to/from other operating, investing, and financing activities, period end accrual adjustments, and reports. Reports include the standard financial statements, including the income statement, statement of stockholders' equity, balance sheet, statement of cash flows, and other useful reports like accounts receivable aging. All interaction with QBO is done via an Internet connection. In other words, if you have not connected to the Internet, you will have no QBO. In other words QBO cannot work offline.

All interaction with QBO is done online, there are no files to maintain on a computer and everything is saved online. Thus, there is no need for backup files. The monthly fee for using QBO covers one and only one company. This text includes access codes for the user to create one company online for a limited amount of time.

How Is QBO Similar/Different than the Desktop Version QuickBooks?

Even though these two products share the name "QuickBooks," they are unrelated. QBO isn't a copy of QuickBooks that has been web enabled. They are different products with different database structures and approaches to solving problems even though both were developed in-house by Intuit to capture and report on accounting events.

Not all features available in QBO are available in the Windows desktop version of QuickBooks Accountant (QBDT). Likewise, not all features of QBDT are available in QBO. QBO requires an Internet connection. QBDT requires installation of software on to a computer. QBO requires a monthly fee. QBDT requires a one-time purchase and no monthly fees.

A key difference is that because QBO is online, it works on multiple operating systems (Windows, Apple, etc.) and multiple devices (desktops, laptops, smart phones, or tablets). The same cannot be said for QBDT. Intuit requires different software for QBDT to run on a Windows-based or an Apple-based computer. In this text, QBDT will always mean the Windows version of Quick-Books Accountant.

Some additional notable differences are the following:

* QBDT can be used for an unlimited number of companies; QBO limits you to one company per license fee. Need to manage more than one company using QuickBooks? Each will cost you another monthly fee.

* QBO can automatically download bank transactions for no additional cost.

* QBDT can track inventory purchases and sales based on an average cost assumption or a first-in-first-out assumption.

* QBO can track inventory purchases and sales based only on a first-in-first-out assumption.

* QBDT can account for the receipt of inventory items (receive items function) based on a purchase order; QBO cannot and calls inventory products and services.

* QBO can automatically schedule and send invoices whereas QBDT cannot.

* QBDT can perform manual payroll without paying Intuit a monthly payroll processing fee. QBO encourages you to sign up for its payroll service and makes manually processing payroll difficult.

* QBO can be accessed from anywhere in the world where you have access to the Internet. QBDT requires a computer with the QuickBooks application and data files installed.

* QBDT provides for profit and loss as well as balance sheet budgeting. QBO only provides for profit and loss budgeting.

* QBO operates irrespective of platform (desktop, laptop, mobile device, or tablet) or operating system (Microsoft Windows or Apple iOS). QBDT does have a version of QuickBooks for both of those operating systems, but they are different and require two separate application purchases.

- QBDT includes a fixed asset management, which will calculate depreciation and maintain detailed fixed asset records by individual asset, whereas QBO does not calculate depreciation and does not maintain detailed records of fixed assets.

- QBO provides automatic upgrades; this is a good and a bad feature. With QuickBooks Online, you are almost always running the most current version (whether you want to or not).

Creating a New QBO Account

Before getting started, you will need to establish your account with QBO. This text includes access codes for one user. Once you use the codes, they will not work again.

To launch QBO and create a new account, do the following:

1 Open your Internet browser.

2 Type **https://quickbooks.intuit.com/start/retail_sui** into your browser's address text box.

3 Type your license number and product number (provided with the text) shown in Figure 1.1.

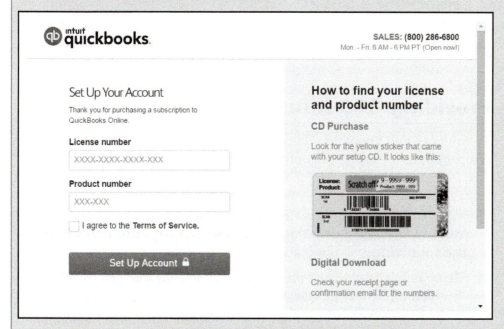

Figure 1.1

Set Up Your Account window

4 Click the **I agree to the Terms of Service** check box and then click **Set Up Account**.

5 Enter information about you as shown in Figure 1.2, changing all the information to your first and last name, your email address (user id), and password, then click **Create Account**.

Figure 1.2

Setting Up Your Account

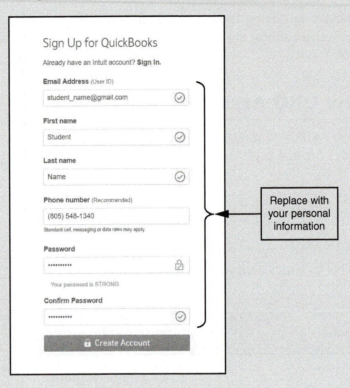

Providing QBO Information

To continue, QBO requires additional information, such as the industry your company operates, the types or products you sell, etc.

To provide QBO additional information (continuing from above), do the following:

1 Type your name and your identification number as specified by your instructor to answer the question "What is your business called?". Then select **Less than one year** to answer the question "How long have you been in business?". Then click **Next**.

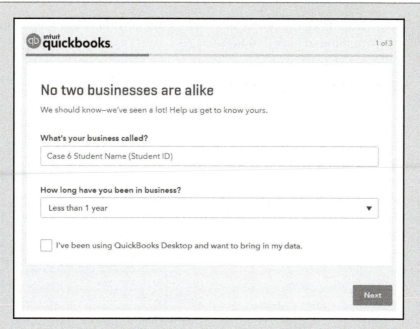

Figure 1.3

Basic Info window

2 Do not select any option buttons when asked what one thing QuickBooks can help you with today, then click **Next**.

3 Select the **Send and track invoices, Organize your expenses, Manage your inventory, Track the products you sell, Track your bills, Track your sales tax**, and **Pay your employees** buttons as shown in Figure 1.4 then click **All set**.

Figure 1.4

Choose Options in QBO

4   Scroll down the home page to hide the tutorial steps. The home page should now look like Figure 1.5.

Figure 1.5

Home Page (partial view)

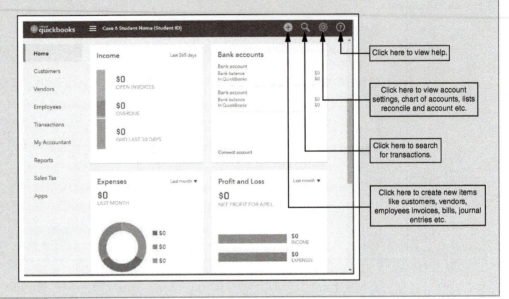

Navigating QBO

The Home page (soon to be called the Dashboard) provides links to various tasks and resources. The Customers window provides access to adding new customers, viewing existing balances, and highlighting overdue accounts. The Vendors window provides access to adding new vendors, viewing existing balances, and highlighting overdue accounts. The Employees window provides access to adding new employees and viewing payroll information. The Transactions and Reports links will be addressed later in this text. To begin, you should access QBO's help features.

To use QBO help:

1   Click the **?** button located in the upper-right portion of your window. Click the text **Home page overview** to open a window shown in Figure 1.6.

Figure 1.6

Home Page Overview

Home page overview

Welcome to the Intuit QuickBooks Home page! The Home page is where you go for an overview of your company and primary activities.

From the Home page, you can:

- Get going quickly! Create your first invoice, add your first expenses, and connect your bank and credit card accounts
- Use the Create (+) menu to do typical tasks
- See a simple snapshot of your finances
- View recent activity and transactions

When you're ready to go beyond the basics, you can:

- Configure company settings
- Search for transactions
- Manage users and their access
- Change your user ID and password
- Edit contact and sign-in information

2   Click the text **Use the Create (+) menu to do typical tasks** to view Figure 1.7.

Figure 1.7

Using the Create (+) menu

Use the Create (+) menu to do typical tasks

To display a menu of frequent tasks, click **Create (+)** at the top of the page. If you don't see a necessary menu item, click **Show more** to show more options.

You can also click the **Gear icon** at the top right. This displays a menu of areas that you use less often, such as **Company Settings** (or **Account and Settings** depending on what you see), **Chart of Accounts**, and **Manage Users**.

3   Close the help window, and then click the **Create +** menu at the top of the Home page to view the full create menu items available as shown in Figure 1.8.

Figure 1.8

The Create (+) menu

Create

Customers	Vendors	Employees	Other
Invoice	Expense	Payroll	Bank Deposit
Receive Payment	Check	Single Time Activity	Transfer
Estimate	Bill	Weekly Timesheet	Journal Entry
Credit Memo	Pay Bills		Statement
Sales Receipt	Purchase Order		Inventory Qty Adjustment
Refund Receipt	Vendor Credit		
Delayed Credit	Credit Card Credit		
Delayed Charge	Print Checks		

4 Click **Customers** from the navigation bar on the left of the Home page to view Figure 1.9. Since you have not yet entered any customers, QBO will ask you to add your first customer. You will do this later in Chapter 3. Remember QBO is an online application and Intuit will change it often. Thus the figures in this text may differ from what you see in QBO online.

Figure 1.9

Customers window

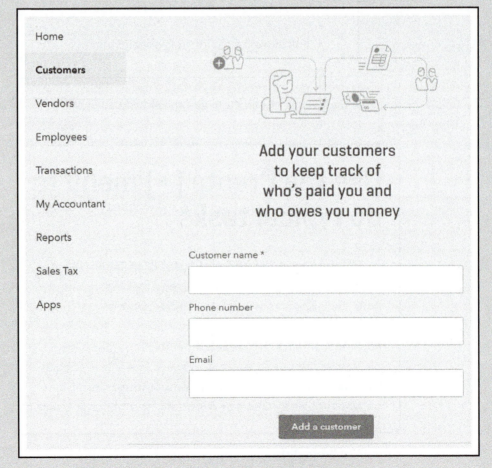

5 Click **Vendors** from the navigation bar on the left of the Home page to view Figure 1.10.

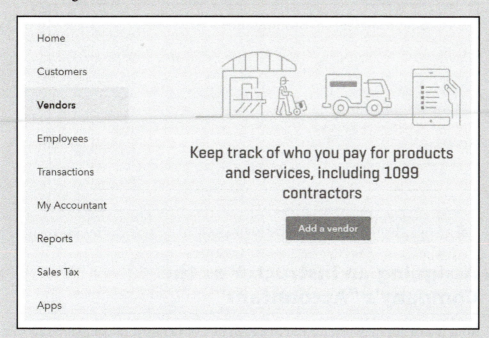

Figure 1.10

Vendors window

6 Click **Employees** from the navigation bar on the left of the Home page to view Figure 1.11.

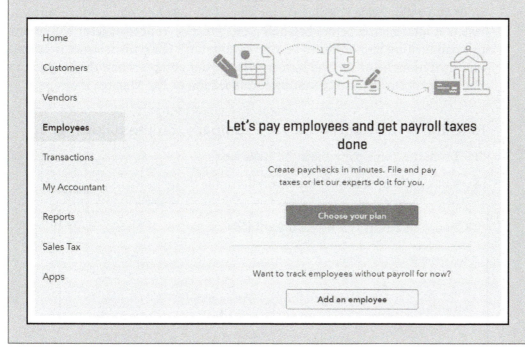

Figure 1.11

Employees window

7 Click the **Gear** icon located in the upper-right corner of the Home page to view Figure 1.12.

Figure 1.12

Gear window

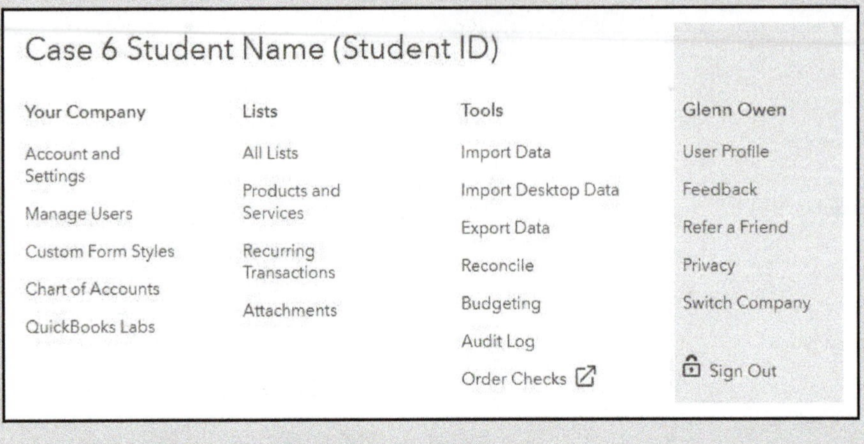

Case 6 Student Name (Student ID)

Your Company	Lists	Tools	Glenn Owen
Account and Settings	All Lists	Import Data	User Profile
Manage Users	Products and Services	Import Desktop Data	Feedback
Custom Form Styles	Recurring Transactions	Export Data	Refer a Friend
Chart of Accounts	Attachments	Reconcile	Privacy
QuickBooks Labs		Budgeting	Switch Company
		Audit Log	
		Order Checks	Sign Out

8 Click **Home** to return to the Home page.

Assigning an Instructor as the Company's "Accountant"

Your instructor may require you to assign him or her as your company's accountant. You do this so he or she, as your accountant, will always have access to your company files for grading and evaluation purposes. This will also assist the instructor in answering questions you may have about your company. The process of assigning an accountant to your company involves a brief interview in which you will provide your instructor's email address and name. Make sure you have that information before beginning this process. Your instructor will receive an email inviting him or her to be your accountant. Once the instructor accepts your invitation, he or she will have access to your company and the instructor's name will appear in the Accounting Firms section of the Manage Users page.

To assign an accountant to your company, do the following:

1 From the home page, click the **Gear** icon.

2 Click **Manage Users** shown in Figure 1.13.

Figure 1.13

Gear window (Manage Users option)

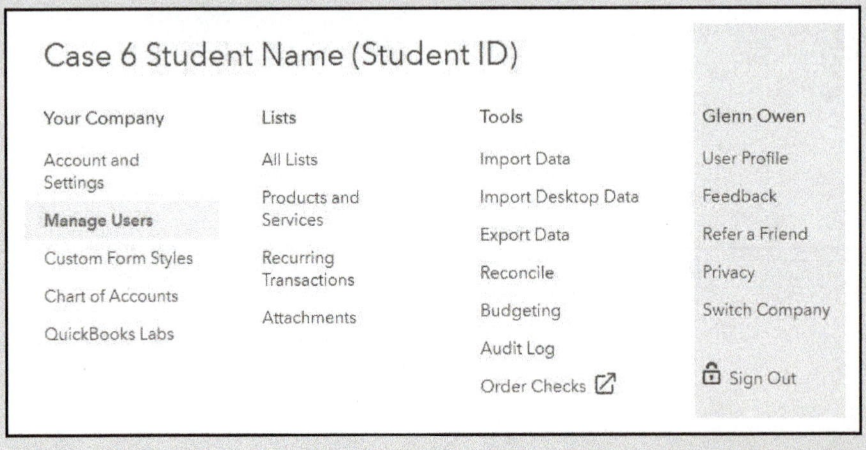

Case 6 Student Name (Student ID)

Your Company	Lists	Tools	Glenn Owen
Account and Settings	All Lists	Import Data	User Profile
Manage Users	Products and Services	Import Desktop Data	Feedback
Custom Form Styles	Recurring Transactions	Export Data	Refer a Friend
Chart of Accounts	Attachments	Reconcile	Privacy
QuickBooks Labs		Budgeting	Switch Company
		Audit Log	
		Order Checks	Sign Out

3　Click **Invite Accountant** shown in Figure 1.14. A new Mini Interview window will appear.

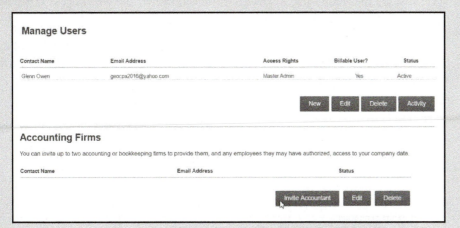

Figure 1.14

Manage Users window
(inviting instructor as accountant)

Figure 1.14

Manage Users window
(inviting instructor as accountant)

4　Type your instructor's email address and name in the space provided and click **Next** shown in Figure 1.15.

Figure 1.15

Accountant's information
(instructor information to QBO)

5　Click **Finish**.

Using QBO's Help Feature

QBO provides help with a handy search feature. Help comes in two forms: built-in from Intuit and dynamic help from the QuickBooks Community.

To access Help from within QBO, do the following:

1 Click **?** located in the upper right of the Home page to access QBO help. (In fact, help is available on all windows.)

2 Type **chart of accounts** in the search box of the Help window to see available help shown in Figure 1.16. *Trouble!* Be quick because if you wait too long, QBO will revert to the Top help topics list.

Figure 1.16

Help window
(searching chart of accounts)

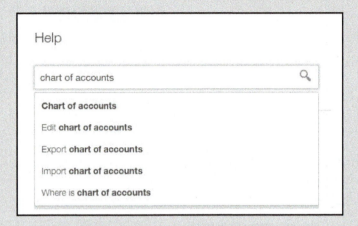

3 Click the text **Where is chart of accounts** to view Figure 1.17. *Trouble!* Be quick because if you wait too long, QBO will revert to the Top help topics list. If this happens, retype chart of accounts in the search box.

Figure 1.17

Help window
(searching chart of accounts location)

4 Scroll down the help window and then click the text **Review your chart of accounts** to view a QuickBooks Help response shown in Figure 1.18. Because this is a dynamic help and may change daily, your window may differ.

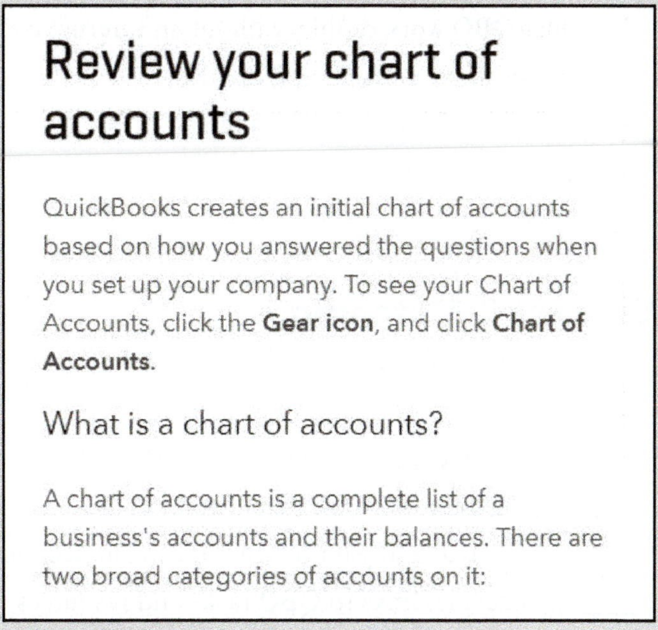

Figure 1.18

Help window (answer)

Review your chart of accounts

QuickBooks creates an initial chart of accounts based on how you answered the questions when you set up your company. To see your Chart of Accounts, click the **Gear icon**, and click **Chart of Accounts**.

What is a chart of accounts?

A chart of accounts is a complete list of a business's accounts and their balances. There are two broad categories of accounts on it:

5 Close the Help Answer window.

6 Click the **Gear** icon and click **Sign Out**.

End Note

You have now been introduced to QBO, its basic features, and how it is similar to but not the same as QBDT. You created your Intuit account and provided basic information about your company and learned how to navigate around the QBO application. After assigning your instructor as your accountant and learning more about the help features in **QBO**, you are ready to learn more about the application by exploring a sample company provided by Intuit in Chapter 2. Don't worry because you will be back to your company in Chapter 3.

Chapter 1 Questions

1 How are QBO and QBDT different in the number of companies they can manage per license?

2 Does QBO work offline, without an Internet connection?

3 Do you need to back up QBO files?

4 How are QBO and QBDT similar?

5 What information do you need to supply to assign your instructor as the company's accountant?

Chapter 1 Matching

a. QBO

b. QBDT

c. Gear icon

d. Welcome Guide

e. Navigation bar

f. Create (+) icon

g. Magnifying Glass

h. Help (?) icon

i. Manage Users

j. Home page

_____ Click to access help

_____ Click to find past transactions

_____ Provides tasks to help you get started

_____ Online version of QuickBooks

_____ Click to add your instructor as your accountant

_____ Provides links to QBO tasks and resources

_____ Windows Desktop version of QuickBooks

_____ Click to add any transaction

_____ Click to manage your subscription, users, and settings

_____ On the left of the Home page, it shows a menu of items

Sample Company Walkthrough

2

Student Learning Outcomes

Upon completion of this chapter, the student will be able to do the following:

- Open the Sample Company provided by Intuit to explore QBO
- Access customer, vendor, and employee information
- Explore banking transactions
- Explore sales and expense transactions
- Explore the chart of accounts
- Explore lists
- Access reports
- Use the Gear icon to view company settings

Overview

Intuit has provided a Sample Company online to provide new users a test drive of its QBO product. You will open this Sample Company and explore various features of QBO. In this chapter, you will be viewing the Sample Company looking at customer, vendor, and employee information. You will also be viewing banking, sales, and expense transactions and will be looking at the chart of accounts, lists, reports, and company settings. You will not be making any changes, such as adding a customer, invoice, check, etc. That will occur in the next chapter.

The author has no control over the dates used by Intuit, and those dates may change, depending on when you are accessing the file online. The dates that appear in the figures supplied by the author in this text may not be the dates that appear on your screen.

Begin Your Sample Company Walkthrough

You can use this Sample Company to explore QBO as often as you like. No matter what you do to modify this Sample Company, you will be unable to save it. When you leave and later return, it will look the same as it did initially. Each time you open this Sample Company, it will retrieve your current system date (the actual date you are working on your computer) and place that date under the company name on the home page.

To open the Sample Company, do the following:

1 Open your Internet browser.

2 Type **https://qbo.intuit.com/redir/testdrive** into your browser's address text box, and press [**Enter**] to view the Sample Company Home page shown in Figure 2.1. You may be asked to provide security information before proceeding. If so, type the words provided into the text box and click **Continue**. Your system date will differ from the date shown under the company name in the following figure. Transaction dates may also differ on your screen from the figures shown throughout this text.

Figure 2.1

Sample Company Home page

Note that the Navigation bar in this figure has a black background and the current version of QBO has no background. Get used to cosmetic changes that Intuit makes with QBO that don't affect its functionality but do affect its look.

In Chapter 1, you used the Welcome Guide to better acquaint yourself with the Home page. The Find your way around section of the Welcome Guide is shown next in Figure 2.2 as a reminder. As you explore the navigation bar, you will be directed to right-click tasks so they open up in a new tab in your browser. This will facilitate viewing multiple sections of QBO easily.

Figure 2.2

Find your way around (Home page overview)

Customers, Vendors, and Employees

QBO provides easy access to customer information using the navigation bar. In this section, you will open the Customers section in a new tab and drill down to a specific customer, and specific transactions relate to that customer.

To access customer information, do the following:

1 Right click **Customers** from the navigation bar and select **Open link in new tab** shown in Figure 2.3.

Figure 2.3

Home page (right click to view Customers in a new tab)

2 Click on the new **Customers** tab. Your window should look like Figure 2.4.

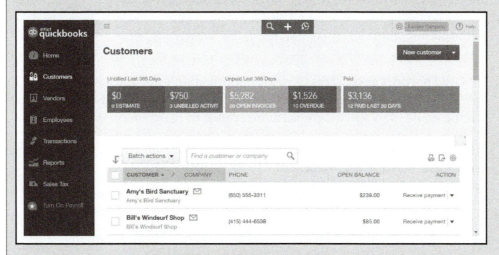

Figure 2.4

Customers window

3 Click on the text **Amy's Bird Sanctuary** to view detail transactions related to that particular customer shown in Figure 2.5

Figure 2.5

Amy's Bird Sanctuary

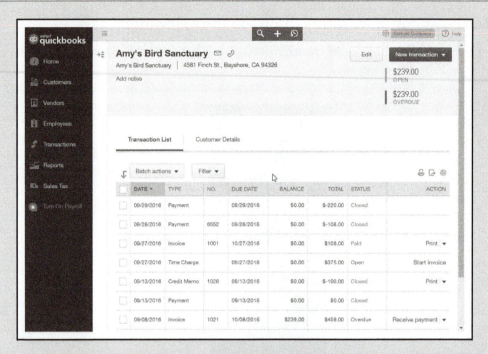

The $239.00 overdue balance noted at the top of the window correlates to invoice 1021 shown near the bottom of the figure. (The author has no control over the dates used by Intuit, and those dates may change depending on when you are accessing the file online. The dates, which appear in the figures supplied by the author in this text, may not match the dates that appear on your screen.)

QBO provides easy access to vendor information using the navigation bar. In this section, you will open the Vendors section in a new tab and drill down to a specific vendor and specific transactions related to that vendor.

To access vendor information, do the following:

1 Right click **Vendors** from the navigation bar and select **Open link in new tab**. The resulting action will add a new tab to your browser.

2 Click on the new **Vendors** tab to reveal a Vendor listing shown in Figure 2.6.

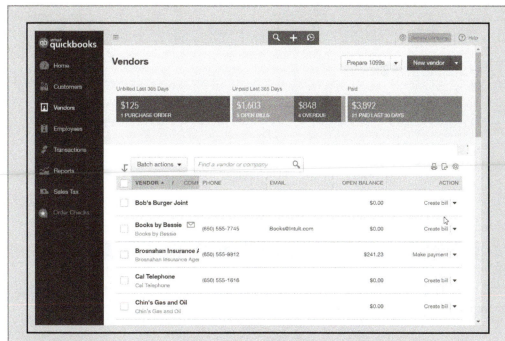

Figure 2.6

Vendors information

3 Click on the text **Brosnahan Insurance Agency** to view detail transactions related to that particular vendor shown in Figure 2.7

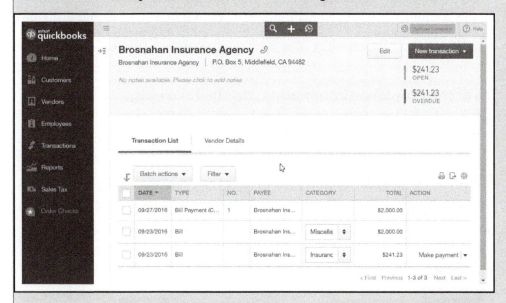

Figure 2.7

Brosnahan Insurance Agency

4 Double click on the **$241.23** balance to view the bill received and shown in Figure 2.8.

Figure 2.8

Bill from Brosnahan Insurance Agency

The $241.23 overdue balance noted at the top of the window correlates to a bill received from an earlier month.

QBO provides easy access to employee information using the navigation bar. In this section, you will open the Employees section in a new tab and drill down to a specific employee and specific transactions related to that employee.

To access employee information, do the following:

1   Click on the **X** in the upper right corner of the Bill to close it and then right-click **Employees** from the navigation bar and then select **Open link in new tab**. The resulting action will add a new tab to your browser.

2   Click on the new **Employees** tab to reveal an Employee listing shown in Figure 2.9.

Figure 2.9

Employees information

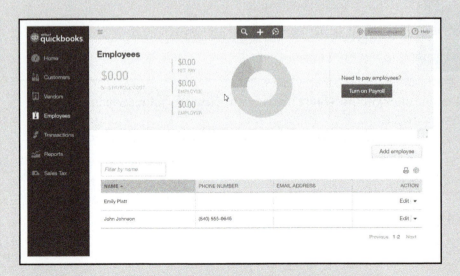

1 Click on the text **Edit** for John Johnson to view employee information for John Johnson shown in Figure 2.10.

Figure 2.10

Employee Information for John Johnson

2 Click **Cancel** to close this window.

3 Click the **Gear** icon, and click **Sign Out** to close the Sample Company.

Banking Transactions

QBO has an online banking feature that lets you automatically connect to your bank and download banking-related transactions. The application automatically matches the banking transaction with a previously recorded QBO transaction. QBO calls this "Recognizing." This feature is briefly reviewed since this text is academically based and no "real" bank account is linked to this sample and no "real" bank account will be linked to your student company.

To view banking transactions, do the following:

1 Open your Internet browser.

2 Type **https://qbo.intuit.com/redir/testdrive** into your browser's address text box and then press [**Enter**] to view the Sample Company Home page shown in Figure 2.1. You may be asked to provide security information before proceeding. If so, type the words provided into the text box and then click **Continue**.

3 Click **Transactions** and then click **Banking** from the Navigation Bar on the home page to view the **Bank and Credit Cards** page of the Sample Company.

4   Select **Checking** from the drop-down menu at the top of the window to view the window shown in Figure 2.11.

Figure 2.11

Bank and Credit Cards (partial view)

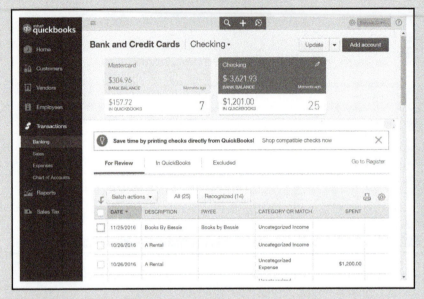

5   Click the **Recognized** (14) tab to view the listing of only those banking transactions recognized by QBO shown in Figure 2.12.

Figure 2.12

Bank and Credit Cards (recognized banking transactions: partial view)

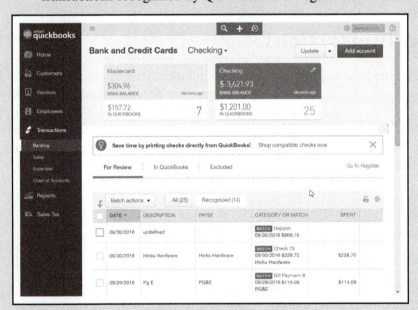

6   Click **Go to Register** on the right to view the traditional checking account register listing each QBO recorded check, deposit, or cash transaction affecting the checking account shown in Figure 2.13. Close any messages that may appear. You may have to enlarge your window to view the Deposit and Balance columns.

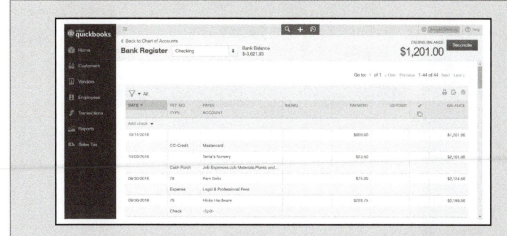

Figure 2.13

Bank Register (partial view)

Bank deposits, which have not been recorded in QBO, are not recognized and are temporarily classified as Uncategorized Income. Bank charges that have not been recorded in QBO are not recognized and are temporarily classified as Uncategorized Expense.

The Register seen in Figure 2.13 is similar to the general ledger account concept seen in traditional accounting without the debits and credits. The balance is shown after every increase or decrease in the account. In a bank account, increases are deposits and decreases are payments. Registers exist for all asset, liabilities, and equity accounts and are a great way to identify and/or correct errors if they occur.

Sales and Expense Transactions

The next two choices in the navigation bar are sales and expenses transactions. The sales transaction section will provide a listing of recent sales invoices and payments: Some are closed and others are open, meaning payment has not been received. Thus, the action of receiving payment is listed for all open invoices. This screen also highlights unbilled activity, open balances, overdue balances, and those invoices paid in the last 30 days across the top. You can decide to drill down to view a particular invoice.

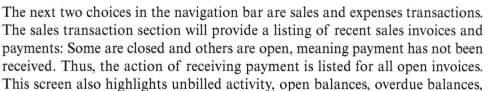

To view sales and expenses transactions, do the following:

1 Click **Transactions** and then click **Sales** from the navigation bar to view the Sales section shown in Figure 2.14.

Figure 2.14

Sales Transactions (partial view)

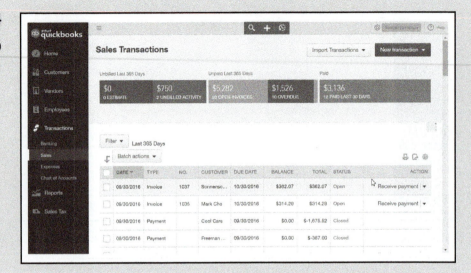

2 Double click on Invoice No. **1035** to reveal the invoice shown in Figure 2.15.

Figure 2.15

Invoice # 1035

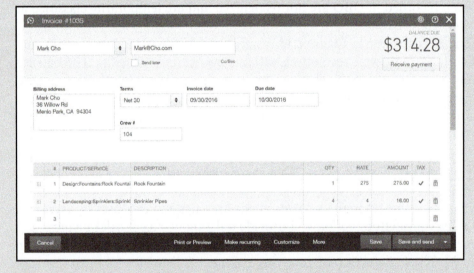

3 Click **Cancel** to close Invoice No. 1035.

The expenses section will provide a listing of recent credit card transactions, bills, expenses, purchase orders, checks, bill payments, and cash transactions. You can decide to drill down to view a particular credit card transaction.

4 Click **Transactions** and then click **Expenses** from the navigation bar to view the Expense Transactions section shown in Figure 2.16.

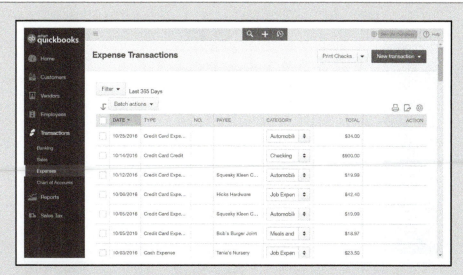

Figure 2.16

Expense Transactions (partial view)

5 Double click the Credit Card Expense for $19.99 with payee **Squeaky Kleen Car Wash** to reveal the charge shown in Figure 2.17.

Figure 2.17

Expense window (credit card charge for $19.99)

6 Click **Cancel** to close the credit card charge window.

Chart of Accounts

A chart of accounts is a listing of all accounts available. Each account is assigned a type and a detailed type. The Sample Company's chart of accounts has been modified from the default chart of accounts and tailored to this company's needs. Not all companies need these particular accounts, and some will need additional accounts.

To view the Sample Company's chart of accounts, do the following:

1 Click **Transactions** and then click **Chart of Accounts** from the navigation bar to view the Chart of Accounts section shown in Figure 2.18.

Figure 2.18

Chart of Accounts (partial view)

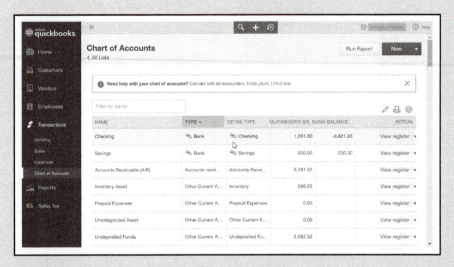

2   Scroll down the chart of accounts. Each asset, liability, and equity account has a View Register action item listed.

3   As you scroll down, you will see that the balance in the chart of accounts for accounts payable (A/P) is $1,602.67.

4   Click **View Register** on the Accounts Payable line of the chart of accounts to view the Register for accounts payable shown in Figure 2.19. The ending balance in the A/P Register matches the $1,602.67 balance specified in the chart of accounts listing. (Remember to ignore dates in this Sample problem.)

Figure 2.19

A/P Register

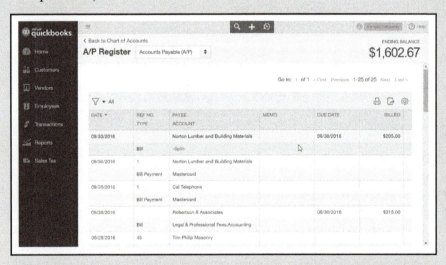

5   Click **Back to Chart of Accounts** located at the top of the A/P Register.

6   Scroll down the chart of accounts to see that each revenue and expense account has a Run Report action item listed. Click on **Run Report** on the Landscaping Service account line to view an Account Quickreport for the Landscaping Services account.

7   In the Transaction Date text box, click the drop-down list and select **This Year-to-date,** and then click **Run Report** to view the report shown in Figure 2.20.

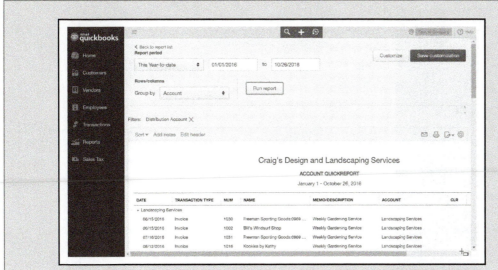

Figure 2.20

Account Quickreport

Lists

Lists in QBO provide you with an easy and quick way to view a collection of common items. Some of the more common lists include the chart of accounts, products and services, and terms. You can decide to view a summary of all the lists available in QBO and explore the list of terms.

To view a list of lists and the list of terms, do the following:

1 Click the **Gear** icon and then click **All Lists** to view a list of lists shown in Figure 2.21.

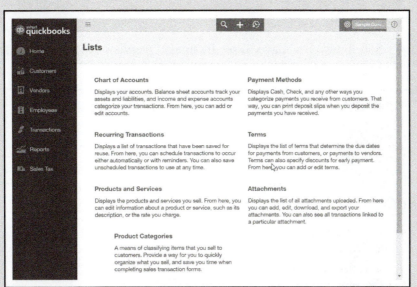

Figure 2.21

Lists

2 Click **Terms** to view the list shown in Figure 2.22.

Figure 2.22

Terms

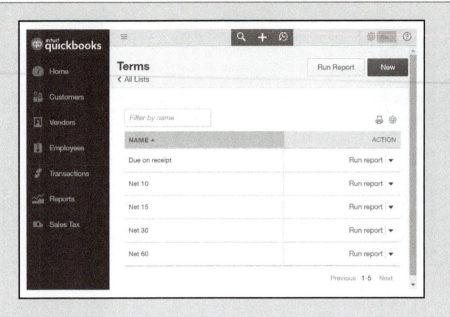

Reports

QBO comes with many predesigned reports for use in business, all of which you can customize for your particular needs. For instance, you can decide to focus on the common financial statement reports: the Income Statement (known in QBO as the Profit and Loss report), Balance sheet, and Statement of Cash Flows.

1 Click **Reports** from the navigation bar.

2 Click **All Reports**.

3 Click **Business Overview**.

4 Scroll down the page to see Business Overview report options shown in Figure 2.23.

Figure 2.23

Business Overview reports

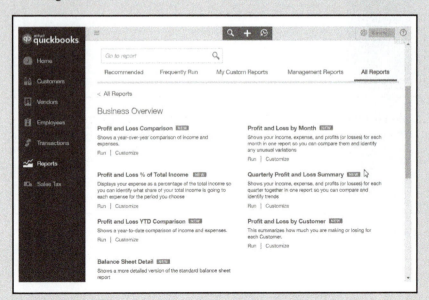

5 Scroll down to find and click **Profit and Loss**. Click **Collapse** to view the report shown in Figure 2.24. (If you view the entire report you would note that clicking the **Collapse** text summarizes details under a heading. For example, Landscaping Services is shown as one number when Collapse is selected. Clicking **Expand** would show more detail. You will learn more about customizing and creating other reports in Chapter 10. Remember, the dates on your screen may differ from those shown in the figure.)

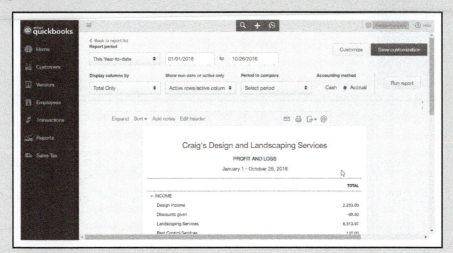

Figure 2.24

Profit and Loss report

6 Click **Reports** and then scroll down to find and click **Balance Sheet** to view the Balance Sheet report shown in Figure 2.25.

Figure 2.25

Balance Sheet (partial view)

7 Click **Reports** and then scroll down to find and click **Statement of Cash Flows** to view the Statement of Cash Flows report shown in Figure 2.26.

Figure 2.26

Statement of Cash Flows

Alternatively, you can easily find a report if you know its name or part of its name. For example, if you wanted to access a report dealing with accounts receivable (A/R), you would type A/R into the report search box located in the Reports section.

To find a report related to accounts receivable, do the following:

1   Click **Reports** and type A/R in the Reports search box shown in Figure 2.27.

Figure 2.27

Reports

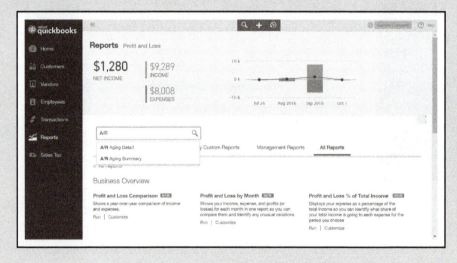

Company Settings

Four tabs are in the Settings section of QBO: Company, Sales, Expenses, and Advanced. You can edit these by clicking on the Pencil icon to the right of each section. The settings for the Sample Company have been modified from the default settings provided when QBO first creates a company. These options in the Settings section change the way QBO appears to the user. For example, in the Advanced section, if time tracking is turned off, no time tracking features will be available in QBO. Also, if purchase orders are turned off in the Expenses section, no purchase orders will be available in QBO. You can decide to view each of these sections to learn more about what options you are given in QBO.

1 Click the **Gear** icon and then click **Account and Settings** and click the **Company** tab to view the company settings section shown in Figure 2.28.

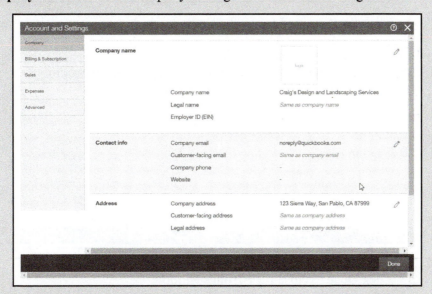

Figure 2.28

Company settings

2 Click the **Sales** tab in the **Settings** window to view options provided shown in Figure 2.29.

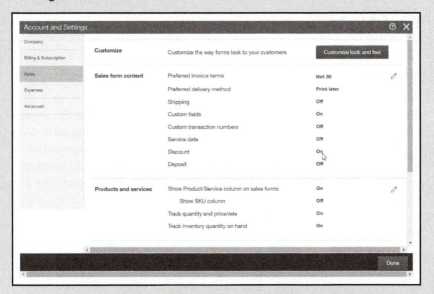

Figure 2.29

Sales settings

3 Click the **Expenses** tab in the **Settings** window to view options provided shown in Figure 2.30.

Figure 2.30

Expenses settings

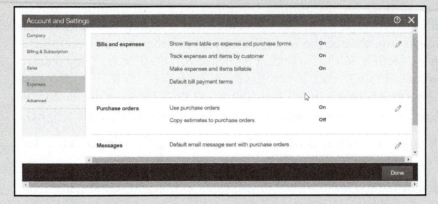

4 Click the **Advanced** tab in the **Settings** window to view options provided shown in Figure 2.31.

Figure 2.31

Advanced settings

5 Click **Done** to close the **Settings** window.

End Note

In this chapter, you have used Intuit's Sample Company to practice navigating QBO. You have accessed customer, vendor, and employee information; viewed various transactions; and viewed the chart of accounts, lists, reports, and company settings. In Chapters 4 through 10, you will use the same Sample Company to learn how to add operating, investing, and financing activities; reconcile a bank account; create a budget; add adjusting entries; and prepare financial statements and reports. In Chapter 3, you will return to your company and modify default settings; add new accounts and beginning balances; and add customers, vendors, products, and services.

Chapter 2 Questions

1   What steps do you take to view customer information in a new tab?

2   What steps do you take to view detail transactions related to a particular customer?

3   What steps do you take to view a specific bill from a specific vendor?

4   What steps do you take to view a specific employee's information?

5   How are bank deposits, which have not been recorded in QBO, classified?

6   How are bank charges, which have not been recorded in QBO, classified?

7   Opening the sales transaction section of QBO will provide a listing of _____.

8   Opening the expense transaction section of QBO will provide a listing of _____.

9   What lists are available in QBO?

10 What steps do you take to view all reports related to accounts payable (A/P)?

Chapter 2 Matching

a. Navigation bar   _____ An employee in the Sample Company

b. Amy's Bird Sanctuary   _____ Bank deposits not yet recognized

c. Brosnahan Insurance Agency _____ Exist for all asset, liability, and equity accounts

d. Recognizing   _____ Specify due dates for payment to/from vendors/customers

e. Uncategorized Income   _____ Used to access a list of sales and expense transactions

f. Uncategorized Expense   _____ A vendor in the Sample Company

g. Registers   _____ A listing of all accounts available

h. John Johnson   _____ Bank charges not yet recognized

i. Terms   _____ A customer in the Sample Company

j. Chart of accounts   _____ Matching a banking transaction with a QBO transaction

3

Setting Up a New Company

Student Learning Outcomes

Upon completion of this chapter, the student will be able to do the following:

- Log into their account
- Change company settings
- Modify the chart of accounts; establish beginning balances; and create new customers, vendors, products, and services
- Close opening balance equity and create a balance sheet
- Create, print, and export a transaction detail by account report

Overview

You began this process in Chapter 1 when you created your account and provided basic information about your company including the company name, address, industry, type, etc. Now it's time to continue that process.

First off, however, you're going to revisit the sample company you worked on in Chapter 2. Each of the following chapters will work the same way. To begin, you will navigate your browser to the Intuit Sample Company. The text will demonstrate how to do certain tasks, such as modify defaults, add a new account, add a new transaction, etc. These demonstrations will occur in the Sample Company. Remember, you can modify the Sample Company throughout each session, but once you close your browser window, QBO will not remember any of your activity in the Sample Company. When you navigate your browser back to the sample company, it will appear as it first did.

Each section of every chapter will begin with a demonstration using the Sample Company. That is followed by you logging back into QBO with the user name and password you created in Chapter 1 to complete an end of chapter case. In the case, you will be asked to perform tasks similar to those demonstrated in the Sample Company but now in your company. The tasks you accomplish on your company, named "Student Name (ID Number)," are permanent and will be there even after you close your QBO browser window. There is no Save File or Save File As command in QBO. Everything is saved for you.

The dates used in this text for the sample company (Craig's Design and Landscaping Services) coincide with the dates this edition was written (October/November 2016). When you access this sample company (in September of 2017, for example), the transaction dates will be different. Thus the figures in this text and the instructions given specifying dates (like 9/30/2016) need to be altered. The transactions themselves will be the same but their corresponding dates will be different.

Company Settings

You can use this Sample Company to explore QBO as often as you would like. No matter what you do to modify this Sample Company, you will not be able to save it. When you leave and later return, it will look the same as it did initially.

To modify Sample Company settings, do the following:

1   Open your Internet browser.

2   Type **https://qbo.intuit.com/redir/testdrive** into your browser's address text box, and press [**Enter**] to view the Sample Company Home page. The system may ask you to provide security information before proceeding. If so, type the words provided into the text box, and click **Continue**.

3   From the Sample Company home page, click the **Gear** icon to manage your settings shown in Figure 3.1.

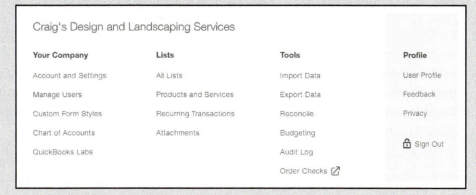

Figure 3.1

Settings

4   Click **Account and Settings**. The first screen shown is the Sample Company information shown in Figure 3.2. Scroll down this page to view information provided and then close this window.

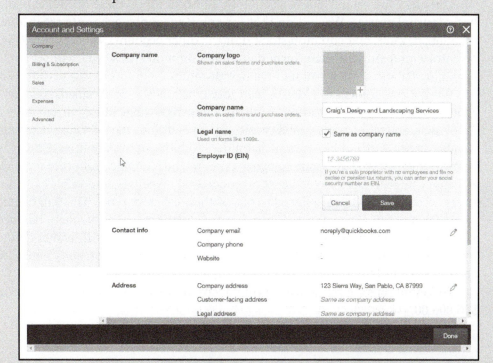

Figure 3.2

Company settings

When you modify the settings of your company, you will visit this section of QBO to make changes and start by selecting the Pencil icon to edit each individual section. You reviewed the four sections of the Company Settings window: Company, Sales, Expenses, and Advanced in Chapter 2. The most common changes to Company Settings involve turning on inventory, tracking of quantities on hand, tracking expenses by customer, making expenses and items billable, establishing default bill payment terms, using purchase orders, and time tracking.

Once you have modified the company settings, it is time to modify the chart of accounts.

Modify the Chart of Accounts and Establish Beginning Balances

You will continue your use of the Sample Company to learn the process of creating, modifying, and deleting accounts and of establishing beginning balances. If you are continuing from above, you will not need to open the Sample Company again. If not, follow the steps above to view the Sample Company. You should complete this entire section in one sitting so you do not lose your work. If you do leave and return, the cumulative balances will be inaccurate as your work will not have been saved while working in the Sample Problem.

Creating accounts and related beginning balances only occurs when you are utilizing QBO for the first time and your business has been in operation for some time. The transition to QBO from a previous accounting system will indicate business events and balances occurred prior to the first date of QBO use.

In this section, you will be adding new checking, inventory, prepaid rent, long-term debt, and common stock accounts to the Sample Company. You will also be establishing beginning balances for checking, accounts receivable, prepaid rent, inventory, and accounts payable. Every time you add a beginning balance, an equal and opposite amount is recorded to the Opening Balance Equity account (to keep debits and credits in balance).

QBO lets you establish a beginning amount for all of these accounts using basic journal entries. We will do that for some accounts, accounts receivable, accounts payable, and common stock. For the other accounts, such as checking, inventory, prepaid rent, long-term debt, and common stock, you will set some beginning balances when you set up a new account.

When a new account is added, its category type needs to be specified. Asset category types include the following: bank, accounts receivable, other current assets, fixed assets, and other assets. Liability category types include the following: accounts payable, credit cards, other current liabilities, and long-term liabilities. Equity is its own category type. Revenue category types include income and other income. Expense category types include cost of goods sold, expenses, and other expense. Every account needs to be assigned to one of these category types. This will dictate where the account appears in all reports, especially the income statement, balance sheet, and statement of cash flows. The detailed category type will further define where the account appears under its category type. Examples of bank category detailed types include cash on hand, checking, money market, and savings.

To begin, let's add a new checking account with a beginning balance of $20,000.00.

To add a new checking account to the chart of accounts and establish a beginning balance, do the following:

1 Click **Transactions** and click **Chart of Accounts** from the Navigation bar.

2 View the chart of accounts. Only one checking account has a Quick-Books balance of $1,201.00.

3 Click the **New** button in the upper right corner of the chart of accounts.

4 Click anywhere in the **Category Type** text box and select **Bank** shown in Figure 3.3.

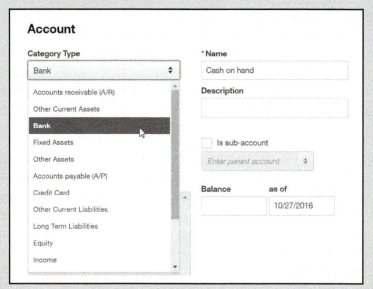

Figure 3.3

Account (adding a new bank account)

5 Select **Checking** from the Detail Type list and type **Checking BOA** in the **Name** text box.

6 Type **20,000.00** in the Balance text box and type **9/30/2016** in the as of text box shown in Figure 3.4 and then press [**Tab**].

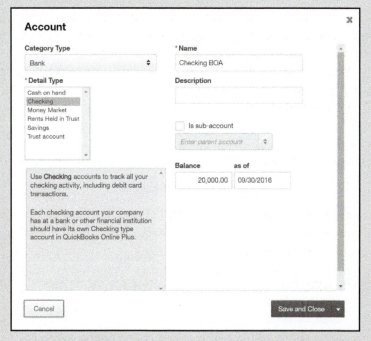

Figure 3.4

Account (completing the addition of a new checking account)

7 Click the **Save and Close** button to view the modified chart of accounts shown in Figure 3.5, which now includes a new checking account with a balance of $20,000.00.

Figure 3.5

Chart of Accounts (modified with the new checking BOA account)

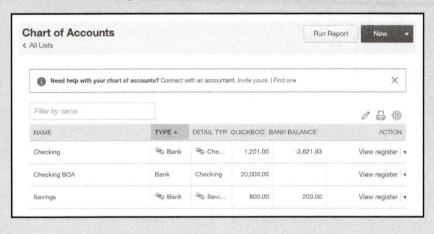

So far, we have added a $20,000 increase to the assets to the Sample Company as of 9/30/16. The Opening Balance Equity account has also increased as the result of this adjustment. To continue, let's add a new product. In QBO, products are merchandise a company purchases from a vendor, maintains in inventory, and then sells to customers. Services are efforts made by a company to add value to a customer. In the Sample Company, an inventory account exists. If you create a new company, an inventory account may not exist. However, when you add a new product, a new inventory account, called inventory asset, will automatically be created.

To add a new product and service, do the following:

1 View the chart of accounts and note the Inventory Asset account with a QuickBooks balance of $596.25.

2 Click the **Gear** icon and click **Products and Services** from the Lists column.

3 Click **New**.

4 Select **Inventory** from the **Select a Product Type** drop-down list.

5 Type **Stone Tile** as the new product in the Name text box.

6 Select **Landscaping** from the Category drop-down list.

7 Type **500** in the **Initial Quantity on Hand** text box and **9/30/2016** in the **As Of Date** text box.

8 Leave **Inventory Asset** as the Inventory Asset Account.

9 Type **Stone Tile** as the description for the Sales and Purchasing information text boxes.

10 Type **2.50** in the Sales price/rate text box and **1.25** in the Cost text box.

11 Leave **Sales of Product Income** as the Income Account and **Cost of Goods Sold** as the Expense Account.

12 Check the **Is taxable** check box. Your window should look like Figure 3.6.

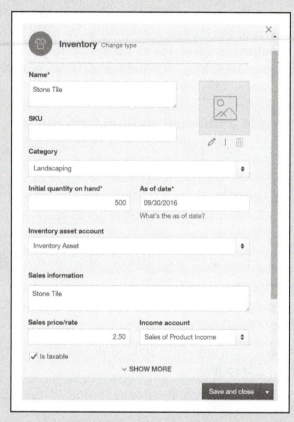

Figure 3.6

Adding Inventory

13 Click the down arrow in the Save and Close button and then select **Save and New.**

14 Click the **change type** text next to the work Inventory at the top of the window. Click **Service.**

15 Type **Estimates** as the name of a new service.

16 Check the **I sell this product/service to my customers** check box.

17 Type **Estimates** as the description in the Sales information text box and then select **Design** from the Category drop-down list.

18 Type **50** in the Sales price/rate text box.

19 Uncheck the **Is taxable** check box and then uncheck the I purchase this product/service from a vendor check box.

20 Click the **Save and Close** button.

21 Scroll down the list of products and services. Note the addition of the new Stone Tile product, with a quantity of 500, and the new Estimates service added.

22 Click **Transactions** and then **Chart of Accounts** from the Navigation Bar and note the new balance in the Inventory Asset account of $1,221.25, which equals the previous balance of 596.25 plus the addition of $625.00 (500 units at the rate of $1.25).

So far, we have added a $20,625 (20,000.00 + 625.00) net increase to the assets to the Sample Company as of 9/30/2016. The Opening Balance Equity account has increased as the result of this adjustment. To continue, let's add prepaid rent, long-term debt, and common stock accounts.

To add additional accounts, do the following:

1 Click the **New** button in the upper right corner of the chart of accounts.

2 Click anywhere in the **Category Type** text box, and select **Other Current Assets.**

3 Select **Prepaid Expenses** as the Detail Type, and type **Prepaid Rent** as the name.

4 Type **4000** in the Balance text box and **9/30/2016** in the **As Of Date** text box.

5 Click the down arrow in the Save and Close button, and select **Save and New**.

6 Click anywhere in the **Category Type** text box, and select **Long Term Liabilities**.

7 Select **Notes Payable** as the Detail Type, and type **Notes Payable Chase** as the name.

8 Type **9000** in the Balance text box and **9/30/2016** in the **As Of Date** text box.

9 Click the down arrow in the Save and Close button, and select **Save and New**.

10 Click anywhere in the **Category Type** text box, and select **Equity.**

11 Select **Common Stock** as the Detail Type, and type **Common Stock** as the name.

12 Type **1000** in the Balance text box and **9/30/2016** in the **As of Date** text box.

13 Click the down arrow in the Save and New button, and select **Save and Close**.

14 Scroll down the chart of accounts. Note the addition of the new Prepaid Rent account with a balance of $4,000.00.

15 Continue scrolling down the chart of accounts. Note the addition of the new Notes Payable Chase account with a balance of $9,000.00.

16 Continue scrolling down the chart of accounts. Note the addition of the new Common Stock account with a balance of $1,000.00.

So far, we have added a $14,625 (20,000 + 625.00 + 4,000.00 − 9,000.00 − 1,000.00) net increase to the assets to the Sample Company as of 9/30/2016. The Opening Balance Equity account is automatically increased as the result of this adjustment.

Lastly, we will set up beginning balances in accounts receivable and accounts payable by using journal entries and add a new customer and vendor at the same time. Journal entries are commonly used to adjust accounts. A customer is an entity to whom you sell products or provide a service. A vendor is an entity from whom you purchase products or services.

To journalize accounts receivable and payable beginning balances, do the following:

1 Before you leave the chart of accounts, note the Opening Balance Equity account that has a balance of $5,287.50.

2 Click the **Create** (+) icon, and click on **Journal Entry** from the Other column.

3 Type **9/30/2016** in the **Journal date** text box.

4 Click in the **Account** column and then click the drop-down arrow.

5 Select **Accounts Receivable (A/R)** as the first account, and type **775** in the Debits column.

6 Click in the Name column, click the drop-down arrow, and select + **Add New** to add a new customer related to this balance shown in Figure 3.7.

Figure 3.7

Accounts Receivable and Payable (journalizing beginning balances)

7 Type **Refugio** as the new customer shown in Figure 3.8.

Figure 3.8

New Name (adding a new customer name)

8   Click **Save** in the New Name box.

9   Select **Accounts Payable (A/P)** as the second account, and type **500** in the Credits column.

10 Click in the **Name** column, click the drop-down arrow, and select **+ Add New** to add a new vendor.

11 Type **Rockster** as the Name, change the Type to **Vendor,** and click **Save**.

12 Select **Opening Balance Equity** as the Account on line 3, and accept 275.00 in the credit column. Your journal entry should look like Figure 3.9.

Figure 3.9

Journal Entry to Set Up A/R and A/P

13 Click **Save and Close** to save your work.

14 Scroll down the chart of accounts, and note the Opening Balance Equity account, which now has a balance of $5,562.50 (5,287.50 + 775.00 − 500.00).

So far, we have added a $14,900 (20,000.00 + 625.00 + 4,000.00 − 9,000.00 − 1,000.00 + 775.00 − 500.00) net increase to the assets to the Sample Company as of 9/30/2016. The Opening Balance Equity account has increased as the result of this adjustment. Additional adjustments were made when Intuit first set this company up. The balance as of 10/1/16 in the Opening Balance Equity account is $5,562.50.

Close Opening Balance Equity and Create a Balance Sheet

The final step in establishing beginning balances in QBO is to close out the Opening Balance Equity account as of 10/1/2016 of $5,562.50. Since we established a common stock account, the only account left in a corporation's equity accounts is retained earnings. Retained earnings are the earnings generated from prior years less dividends. You will need to create a trial balance, which lists the debit or credit balance in all accounts as of a specific date. Your instructor may ask you to customize, print, or export the trial balance to Excel, so you may do that as well.

To close opening balance equity and create, customize, save, print, and export a balance sheet, do the following:

1 Click the **Create (+)** icon, and click on **Journal Entry** from the Other column.

2 Type **10/1/2016** in the **Journal date** text box.

3 Select **Opening Balance Equity** as the first account, and type **5562.50** in the Debits column.

4 Select **Retained Earnings** as the second account, and type **5562.50** in the Credits column. Your journal entry should look like Figure 3.10.

Figure 3.10

Journal Entry #2 (for closing Opening Balance Equity)

5 Click **Save and close**.

6 Click **Reports** in the Navigation Bar.

7 Type **Balance Sheet** into the Go to report search text box, and press [**Enter**].

8 Select **Custom** drop-down list in the Report period text box.

9 Type **10/1/2016** in the **From** text box, and press [**Tab**].

10 Type **10/1/2016** in the **To** text box, and press [**Tab**].

11 Click the **Run Report** button.

12 Click the **printer** icon at the top of the report and then click the **Print** button. Your print out should look like Figure 3.11.

Figure 3.11

Balance Sheet (as of 10/1/2016)

Craig's Design and Landscaping Services
BALANCE SHEET
As of October 1, 2016

	TOTAL
ASSETS	
Current Assets	
Bank Accounts	
Checking	2,124.50
Checking BOA	20,000.00
Savings	800.00
Total Bank Accounts	**$22,924.50**
Accounts Receivable	
Accounts Receivable (A/R)	6,056.52
Total Accounts Receivable	**$6,056.52**
Other current assets	
Inventory Asset	1,221.25
Prepaid Rent	4,000.00
Undeposited Funds	2,062.52
Total Other current assets	**$7,283.77**
Total Current Assets	**$36,264.79**
Fixed Assets	
Truck	
Original Cost	13,495.00
Total Truck	**13,495.00**
Total Fixed Assets	**$13,495.00**
TOTAL ASSETS	**$49,759.79**
LIABILITIES AND EQUITY	
Liabilities	
Current Liabilities	
Accounts Payable	
Accounts Payable (A/P)	2,102.67
Total Accounts Payable	**$2,102.67**
Credit Cards	
Mastercard	922.37
Total Credit Cards	**$922.37**
Other Current Liabilities	
Arizona Dept. of Revenue Payable	0.00
Board of Equalization Payable	370.94
Loan Payable	4,000.00
Total Other Current Liabilities	**$4,370.94**
Total Current Liabilities	**$7,395.98**
Long-Term Liabilities	
Notes Payable	25,000.00
Notes Payable Chase	9,000.00
Total Long-Term Liabilities	**$34,000.00**
Total Liabilities	**$41,395.98**
Equity	
Common Stock	1,000.00
Opening Balance Equity	0.00
Retained Earnings	5,562.50
Net Income	1,801.31
Total Equity	**$8,363.81**
TOTAL LIABILITIES AND EQUITY	**$49,759.79**

13   Click the **Save customization** button.

14   Type **Balance Sheet 10/1/2016** in the Custom report name text box and then select **All** from the Share with drop-down list as shown in Figure 3.12.

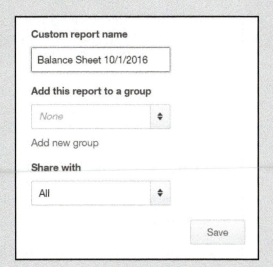

Figure 3.12

Save Report Customizations

15 Click **Save**.

16 Close the print window.

17 Click the **Export** icon shown next to the Printer icon at the top of the report and then select **Export to Excel** from drop-down list to begin the export to Excel process.

18 Type **Balance Sheet** as the file name in the Save As window and then click **Save** after you have navigated to a place on your computer to save this file.

19 Open Excel and then open the file you just saved.

20 After viewing your newly created Excel file, close Excel.

21 Click the **Gear** icon and then click **Sign Out** to exit the sample company.

Create, Print, and Export a Transaction Detail by Account

Often, you will want to investigate a detail list of transactions you have recorded for a specific period. In your end of chapter cases, a usual explanation for an incorrect report is recording a transaction in the incorrect period. To explore this option, you will create a transaction detail by account report for a specific period. You can create such a report for a large period to see if your transactions were recorded in the proper period and to see where you may have entered a wrong amount or account.

To create, print, and export a transaction detail by account report for the period 1/1/2010 to 12/31/2020, do the following:

1   Open your Internet browser.

2   Type **https://qbo.intuit.com/redir/testdrive** into your browser's address text box and the press [**Enter**] to view the Sample Company Home page. All of your transactions from the Sample Company that you recorded in this chapter are gone since you signed out earlier. That's okay.

3   Click **Reports** from the Navigation bar.

4   Type **Transaction** in the Go to Report text box.

5   Select **Transaction Detail by Account.**

6   Select **Custom** from the **Transaction Date** drop-down text box.

7   Type **1/1/2010** in the **From** text box.

8   Type **12/31/2020** in the **To** text box.

9   Click **Run Report**. The top of the report is shown in Figure 3.13.

Figure 3.13

Transaction Detail by Account report (top section)

Craig's Design and Landscaping Services

TRANSACTION DETAIL BY ACCOUNT

January 2010 - December 2020

DATE	TRANSACTION TYPE	NUM	NAME	MEMO/DESCRIPTION	SPLIT	AMOUNT	BALANCE
▾ Checking							
05/18/2016	Deposit			Opening Balance	Opening Balance Equity	5,000.00	5,000.00
06/29/2016	Bill Payment (Check)	10	Robertson & Associates		Accounts Payable (A/P)	-300.00	4,700.00
07/07/2016	Payment	1053	Bill's Windsurf Shop		Accounts Receivable (A/R)	175.00	4,875.00
07/21/2016	Expense	12	Robertson & Associates		Legal & Professional Fees:Accou...	-250.00	4,625.00
08/12/2016	Check	4	Chin's Gas and Oil		Automobile:Fuel	-54.55	4,570.45
08/18/2016	Sales Tax Payment			Q1 Payment	-Split-	-38.50	4,531.95
08/18/2016	Sales Tax Payment			Q1 Payment	-Split-	-38.40	4,493.55
08/21/2016	Expense	9	Tania's Nursery		Job Expenses:Job Materials:Pla...	-89.09	4,404.46
08/21/2016	Check	12	Books by Bessie		Legal & Professional Fees:Bookk...	-55.00	4,349.46
08/27/2016	Check	5	Chin's Gas and Oil		Automobile:Fuel	-62.01	4,287.45
08/28/2016	Expense	15	Tania's Nursery		Job Expenses	-108.09	4,179.36
09/06/2016	Payment	5664	Freeman Sporting Goods:55 Twi...		Accounts Receivable (A/R)	86.40	4,265.76
09/06/2016	Sales Receipt	1008	Kate Whelan		Design income	225.00	4,490.76
09/08/2016	Payment		Amy's Bird Sanctuary	Amy claims the pest control did ...	Accounts Receivable (A/R)	105.00	4,595.76

10   Click on **10** to view the Bill Payment (check) written to Robertson & Associates.

11   Close this window, scroll down the report, and investigate other transactions.

12   Scroll back to the top of this report, and click **Save customization**.

13   Select **All** from the Share with drop-down text box and click **Save**.

14   Click the **Print** button to set this report up for printing; however, do not print this report since it is too long and unnecessary. Click **Cancel**.

15   Click the **Gear** icon and then click **Sign Out**.

End Note

In this chapter, you have logged into your account with QBO, modified company settings, added new accounts to the chart of accounts and added beginning balances where appropriate. You have added customers, vendors, products and services, closed the Opening Balance Equity account and prepared a trial balance. You are ready to add operating activities like sales receipts, invoices, and cash receipts.

Chapter 3 Questions

1 How do you access Company Settings?

2 When is it appropriate to add beginning balances to accounts?

3 What steps need to be followed to add an account to the chart of accounts?

4 When you add a beginning balance to an account, what other account is affected?

5 What information is required when adding a new product to QBO?

6 What additional information is required when you add beginning balance amounts to the accounts receivable account?

7 What additional information is required when you add beginning balance amounts to the accounts payable account?

8 Which additional account is used when you close Opening Balance Equity?

9 How do you access the Balance Sheet report?

10 How can you review a Transactions Report for any account when you are viewing the Balance Sheet?

Chapter 3 Matching

a. Transactions report

b. Trial balance

c. Journal entry

d. Opening Balance Equity

e. Customer

f. Vendor

g. Product

h. Service

i. Category Type

j. Detailed type example

_____ Entity to whom you sell products/services

_____ Account used to offset beginning balances adjustments

_____ Merchandise a company purchases from a vendor

_____ Efforts made by a company to add value to a customer

_____ A listing the debit or credit balances as of a specific date

_____ Dictates where an account appears in all reports

_____ Transactions for an account for a specified period

_____ Entity from whom you purchase products/services

_____ Checking

_____ Commonly used to adjust accounts

Chapter 3 Cases

The following cases require you to open the company you created in Chapter 1. Each of the following cases continues throughout the text in a sequential manner. For example, if you are assigned Case 01, you will use the file you modified in this chapter in all following chapters. Each of the following cases is similar in concepts assessed but differs in amounts and transactions.

To reopen your company, do the following:

1 Open your Internet browser.

2 Type **https://qbo.intuit.com** into your browser's address text box.

3 Type your User ID and Password into the text boxes as shown in Figure 3.14.

Figure 3.14

Sign In Window (for logging in)

Case 1

Your company is a distributor of surfboards located in La Jolla, California. The company does not collect sales tax since all of its customers are resellers. They began business in 2017 and want to use QBO starting January 1, 2018. Beginning balances as of 12/31/2017 have been provided below.

You must make changes to your company. Many settings are set by default. Do not change any settings unless instructed below. Based on what you learned in the text and using the Sample Company, you are to make the following changes:

1 Modify settings as follows:

   a. Company – Company name – Click the Pencil icon to modify the company name to Case 01 – Student Name (ID Number) replacing Student Name with your name and ID Number with the number your instructor indicated.

   b. Sales – Turn on – Track quantity on hand. (This will automatically show items table on expense and purchase forms.)

   c. Expenses –
     i) Turn on – Track expenses and items by customer.
     ii) Turn on – Make expenses and items billable (no markup, track billable expenses and items as income in a single account, no sales tax charged).

iii) Default bill payment terms net 30.

iv) Turn on – Use purchase orders (no custom fields).

    d. Payments – no changes

    e. Advanced

       i) Time tracking

          (1) Turn on – Add Service field to timesheets.

          (2) Turn on – Add Customer field to timesheets.

2 Create new accounts and related beginning balances as follows:

Category Type	Detail Type	Name	Balance	As of
Bank	Checking	Checking	25,000.00	12/31/17
Fixed Assets*	Furniture & Fixtures	Original cost	40,000.00	12/31/17
Fixed Assets*	Furniture & Fixtures	Depreciation	10,000.00	12/31/17
Long-Term Liabilities	Notes Payable	Notes Payable	60,000.00	12/31/17
Equity	Common Stock	Common Stock	1,000.00	12/31/17

*When entering a new fixed asset, place a check in the **Track depreciation of this asset** check box to reveal Original cost and Depreciation text boxes. Enter amounts from above as positive numbers.

3 Create two new products and one new service item as follows:

    a. Products –

       i) Name/Description – Rook 15, track quantity, initial quantity 12/31/17 – 10, inventory asset account – Inventory Asset (this account will automatically be created in the chart of accounts when you add this product), price – $650, cost – $400, income account – Sales, expense account – Cost of Goods Sold.

       ii) Name/Description – The Water Hog, track quantity, initial quantity 12/31/17 – 8, inventory asset account – Inventory Asset, price – $860, cost — $500, income account – Sales, expense account – Cost of Goods Sold.

    b. Service – Name/Description – Consulting, rate – $25, income account – Services

    c. Make changes to the following accounts via journal entry 1 as of 12/31/17 with an offset to Opening Balance Equity:

Account	Amount	Name
Accounts Receivable	5,000.00	Blondie's Boards (new customer)
Prepaid Expenses	3,000.00	
Accounts Payable	4,500.00	Channel Islands (new vendor)

4 Close the Opening Balance Equity account to Retained Earnings via journal entry 2 as of 12/31/17.

5 Prepare and print a Trial Balance report as of 12/31/17, save it as a customized report named Trial Balance 12/31/17, and share it with all users. Your report should look like Figure 3.15.

6 If your trial balance differs from what is in Figure 3.15, do the following:

Figure 3.15

Trial Balance (as of 12/31/17)

Case 1
TRIAL BALANCE
As of December 31, 2017

	DEBIT	CREDIT
Checking	25,000.00	
Accounts Receivable	5,000.00	
Inventory Asset	8,000.00	
Prepaid Expenses	3,000.00	
Furniture & Fixtures:Depreciation		10,000.00
Furniture & Fixtures:Original cost	40,000.00	
Accounts Payable		4,500.00
Notes Payable		60,000.00
Common Stock		1,000.00
Opening Balance Equity		0.00
Retained Earnings		5,500.00
TOTAL	$81,000.00	$81,000.00

    a. Make sure all of your changes were dated 12/31/17.

    b. Click on the debit or credit balance to view a transactions report for each account, and investigate why your answer is different.

    c. Ask your instructor for assistance.

    d. Be sure your company matches the above since, in the following chapter, you will be adding additional business events.

7 Export your Trial Balance report to Excel, and save it with the file name: Student Name (replace with your name) Ch 03 Case 01 Trial Balance. xlsx.

8 Prepare and print a Transaction Detail by Account report for transactions between 1/1/2010 and 12/31/2020, save it as a customized report named Transaction Detail by Account, and share it with all users. If asked, indicate that your business is accrual based.

9 Use your Transaction Detail by Account report to locate any differences in your Trial Balance report created above.

    a. Make sure that all of your changes were dated 12/31/17.

    b. Click on the line that does not match to view the transaction for that account, and investigate why your answer differs.

    c. Ask your instructor for assistance.

    d. Be sure your company matches the above since, in the following chapter, you will be adding additional business events.

10 Export your Transactions Detail by Account report to Excel, and save it with the file name: Student Name (replace with your name) Ch 03 Case 01 Transaction Detail by Account.xlsx.

11 Sign out of your company.

Case 2

Your company is a distributor of remote control toys located in La Jolla, California. The company does not collect sales tax since all of its customers are resellers. They began business in 2018 and want to use QBO starting January 1, 2019. Beginning balances as of 12/31/2018 have been provided below.

You must make changes to your company. Based on what you learned in the text and using the Sample Company, you are to make the following changes:

1 Modify settings as follows:

    a. Company – Company name – Click the Pencil icon to modify the company name to Case 02 – Student Name (ID Number) replacing Student Name with your name and ID Number with the number your instructor indicated.

    b. Sales – Turn on – Track quantity on hand. (This will automatically show items table on expense and purchase forms.)

    c. Expenses –
        i) Turn on – Track expenses and items by customer.
        ii) Turn on – Make expenses and items billable (no markup, track billable expenses and items as income in a single account, no sales tax charged).
        iii) Default bill payment terms net 30.
        iv) Turn on – Use purchase orders (no custom fields).

    d. Payments – no changes

    e. Advanced
        i) Time tracking
            (1) Turn on – Add Service field to timesheets.
            (2) Turn on – Add Customer field to timesheets.

2 Create new accounts and related beginning balances as follows:

Category Type	Detail Type	Name	Balance	As of
Bank	Checking	Checking	5,000.00	12/31/18
Fixed Assets*	Machinery & Equipment	Original cost	10,000.00	12/31/18
Fixed Assets*	Machinery & Equipment	Depreciation	1,000.00	12/31/18
Long-Term Liabilities	Notes Payable	Notes Payable	12,000.00	12/31/18
Equity	Common Stock	Common Stock	100.00	12/31/18

*When entering a new fixed asset, place a check in the **Track depreciation of this asset** check box to reveal Original cost and Depreciation text boxes. Enter amounts from above as positive numbers.

3 Create two new products and one new service item:

   a. Products –

      i) Name/Description – Broon F830 Ride, track quantity, initial quantity 12/31/18 – 4, inventory asset account – Inventory Asset (note: this account will automatically be created in the chart of accounts when you add this product), price – $1,500, cost – $800, income account – Sales, expense account – Cost of Goods Sold.

      ii) Name/Description – Sea Wind Carbon Sailboat, track quantity, initial quantity 12/31/18 – 3, inventory asset account – Inventory Asset, price – $1,200, cost – $620, income account – Sales, expense account – Cost of Goods Sold.

   b. Service – Name/Description – Repairs, rate – $45, income account – Services.

   c. Make changes to the following accounts via journal entry 1 as of 12/31/18 with an offset to Opening Balance Equity:

Account	Amount	Name
Accounts Receivable	925.00	Benson's RC (new customer)
Prepaid Expenses	2,400.00	
Accounts Payable	1,900.00	Kyosho (new vendor)

4 Close the Opening Balance Equity account to Retained Earnings via journal entry 2 as of 12/31/18.

5 Prepare and print a Trial Balance report as of 12/31/18, save it as a customized report named Trial Balance 12/31/18, and share it with all users. Your report should look like Figure 3.16.

Case 2
TRIAL BALANCE
As of December 31, 2018

	DEBIT	CREDIT
Checking	5,000.00	
Accounts Receivable	925.00	
Inventory Asset	5,060.00	
Prepaid Expenses	2,400.00	
Machinery & Equipment:Depreciation		1,000.00
Machinery & Equipment:Original cost	10,000.00	
Accounts Payable		1,900.00
Notes Payable		12,000.00
Common Stock		100.00
Opening Balance Equity		0.00
Retained Earnings		8,385.00
TOTAL	$23,385.00	$23,385.00

Figure 3.16

Trial Balance (as of 12/31/18)

6   If your trial balance is different from what is in Figure 3.16, do the following:

  a. Make sure all of your changes were dated 12/31/18.

  b. Click on the debit or credit balance to view a transactions report for each account, and investigate why your answer is different.

  c. Ask your instructor for assistance.

  d. Be sure your company matches the above since, in the following chapter, you will be adding additional business events.

7   Export your Trial Balance report to Excel, and save it with the file name: Student Name (replace with your name) Ch 03 Case 02 Trial Balance.xlsx.

8   Prepare and print a Transaction Detail by Account report for all transactions between 1/1/2010 and 12/31/2020, save it as a customized report named Transaction Detail by Account, and share it with all users. If asked, indicate that your business is accrual based.

9   Use your Transaction Detail by Account report to locate any differences in your Trial Balance report created above.

  a. Make sure all of your changes were dated 12/31/18.

  b. Click on the line that does not match to view the transaction for that account, and investigate why your answer differs.

  c. Ask your instructor for assistance.

  d. Be sure your company matches the above since, in the following chapter, you will be adding additional business events.

10 Export your Transactions Detail by Account report to Excel and save it with the file name: Student Name (replace with your name) Ch 03 Case 02 Transaction Detail by Account.xlsx.

11 Sign out of your company.

Case 3

Your company sells and services cell phones. They are located in La Jolla, California. The company does collect sales tax since all of its customers are consumers (See Appendix 1 for directions on how to add a sales tax to a company file.) They began business in 2019 and want to use QBO starting January 1, 2020. Beginning balances as of 12/31/2019 have been provided below. You are to make the following changes to the file you created in Chapter 1 based on what you learned in the text using the Sample Company:

1   Modify settings as follows:

  a. Company – Company name – Modify the company name to Case 03 – Student Name (ID Number) replacing Student Name with your name and ID Number with the number your instructor indicated.

  b. SSN – Add 987-65-4321 as your business social security number as you are a sole proprietor.

  c. Sales – Make sure that Track inventory quantity on hand is on. (This will automatically show items table on expense and purchase forms.)

d. Expenses –
    i)   Turn on – Track expenses and items by customer.
    ii) Turn on – Make expenses and items billable (no markup, track billable expenses and items as income in a single account, charge sales tax).
    iii) Set Default bill payment terms to Due on receipt.
    iv) Turn on – Use purchase orders (no custom fields).

e. Payments – no changes

f. Advanced
    i)   Time tracking.
    ii) Turn on – Add Service field to timesheets.
    iii) Turn on – Make Single-Time Activity Billable to Customer.

2 Follow the steps provided in Appendix 1 to add a 10% sales tax titled California, which is payable to the agency titled State Board of Equalization.

3 Create new accounts and related beginning balances (Category Type, Detail Type, Name, Balance as of 12/31/19) as follows:

a. Bank, Checking, Checking, $12,000

b. Fixed Assets, Machinery & Equipment, Original cost, $15,000

    Note: When entering a new fixed asset place a check in the Track depreciation of this asset check box to reveal Original cost and Depreciation text boxes. Enter amounts from above as positive numbers.

c. Fixed Assets, Machinery & Equipment, Depreciation, $2,000

d. Long-Term Liabilities, Notes Payable, Notes Payable, $23,000

e. Equity, Owner's Equity, Owner's Equity, 0

4 Create two new products (Name/Description, initial quantity 12/31/19, inventory asset account, price, cost, income account, expense account):

a. Apple iPhone 7, track quantity, 10, Inventory Asset (Note: This account will automatically be created in the chart of accounts when you add this product), $750, $500, Sales of Product Income, Cost of Goods Sold, taxable.

b. Pixel, track quantity, 3, Inventory Asset, $650, $400, Sales of Product Income, Cost of Goods Sold, taxable.

5 Create two new service items (Name/Description, rate, income account):

a. Apple Repairs, $45, Services, not taxable.

b. Pixel Repairs, $40, Services, not taxable.

6 Add new Account Receivable and Accounts Payable accounts then make changes to the following accounts via journal entry 1 as of 12/31/19 with an offset to Opening Balance Equity:

Account	Amount	Name
Accounts Receivable (A/R)	4,125.00	GHO Marketing (new customer)
Prepaid Expenses	2,750.00	
Accounts Payable (A/P)	5,000.00	Apple Inc. (new vendor)

7 Close the Opening Balance Equity account (which should have a balance of $10, 075) to Owner's Equity via journal entry 2 as of 12/31/19.

8 Prepare and print a Trial Balance report as of 12/31/19, save it as a customized report named Trial Balance 12/31/19, and share it with all users. Your report should look like Figure 3.17.

Figure 3.17

Trial Balance

Case 3 - Student Name (ID number)

TRIAL BALANCE

As of December 31, 2019

	DEBIT	CREDIT
Checking	12,000.00	
Accounts Receivable (A/R)	4,125.00	
Inventory Asset	6,200.00	
Prepaid Expenses	2,750.00	
Machinery & Equipment:Depreciation		2,000.00
Machinery & Equipment:Original cost	15,000.00	
Accounts Payable (A/P)		5,000.00
Notes Payable		23,000.00
Opening Balance Equity		0.00
Owner's Equity		10,075.00
TOTAL	$40,075.00	$40,075.00

9 If your trial balance differs from what is in Figure 3.17, do the following:

a. Make sure all of your changes were dated 12/31/19.

b. Click on the debit or credit balance to view a transactions report for each account, and investigate why your answer is different.

c. Ask your instructor for assistance.

d. Be sure your company matches the above since, in the following chapter, you will be adding additional business events.

10 Export your Trial Balance report to Excel, and save it with the file name: Student Name (replace with your name) Ch 03 Case 03 Trial Balance.xlsx.

11 Prepare and print a Transaction Detail by Account report for all transactions between 1/1/2010 and 12/31/2022, save it as a customized report named Transaction Detail by Account, and share it with all users. If asked, indicate that your business is accrual based.

12 Use your Transaction Detail by Account report to locate any differences in your Trial Balance report created above.

a. Make sure all of your changes were dated 12/31/19.

b. Click on the line that does not match to view the transaction for that account, and investigate why your answer differs.

c. Ask your instructor for assistance.

d. Be sure your company matches the above since, in the following chapter, you will be adding additional business events.

13 Export your Transactions Detail by Account report to Excel and save it with the file name: Student Name (replace with your name) Ch 03 Case 03 Transaction Detail by Account.xlsx.

14 Sign out of your company.

4

Operating Activities: Sales and Cash Receipts

Student Learning Outcomes

Upon completion of this chapter, the student will be able to do the following:

- Create a new service, product, and customer
- Record a sales receipt
- Record an invoice for services rendered on account
- Record an invoice for products sold on account
- Record cash receipts (payments received on account)
- Deposit payments received on account
- Prepare a Transaction Detail by Account report

Overview

Intuit has provided a Sample Company online to provide new users a test drive of its QBO product. In this chapter, you will open this Sample Company and practice various features of QBO. You will be recording operating activities, such as adding new services, new products, new customers, new sales receipts, new invoices, and new cash receipts to the Sample Company file. Remember, if you stop in the middle of this work, none of your work will be saved. So, when you return, the same Sample Company, without your work, will appear. In the end of chapter, you will perform the same tasks completed on the Sample Company on your Student Company. That work of course will be saved.

Services, Products, and Customers

In this section, you will add new services, products, and customers. To add new services and products, you will access the Company section using the **Gear** icon. To add customers, you will use the Customers menu item in the Navigation Bar.

To add new services, products, and customers to the Sample Company, do the following:

1 Open your Internet browser.

2 Type **https://qbo.intuit.com/redir/testdrive** into your browser's address text box and the press [**Enter**] to view the Sample Company Home page. The system may ask you to provide security information before proceeding.

If so, type the words provided into the text box and then click **Continue**. Your system date will differ from the date shown under the company name in the following figure. Transaction dates on your screen may also differ from the figures shown throughout this text.

3 Click the **Gear** icon, and click **Products and Services** shown in Figure 4.1.

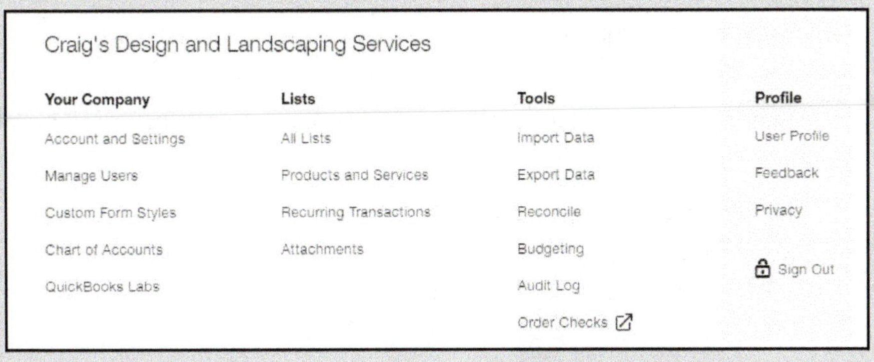

Craig's Design and Landscaping Services

Your Company	Lists	Tools	Profile
Account and Settings	All Lists	Import Data	User Profile
Manage Users	Products and Services	Export Data	Feedback
Custom Form Styles	Recurring Transactions	Reconcile	Privacy
Chart of Accounts	Attachments	Budgeting	
QuickBooks Labs		Audit Log	🔒 Sign Out
		Order Checks 🗗	

Figure 4.1

List of Products and Services

4 Click **New** in the upper right corner of the **Products and Services** list.

5 Click **Select a Product Type** and then select **Service**.

6 Type **Rose Consulting** in the **Name** text box and the **Description on sales forms** text boxes.

7 Check the **Sales Information** check box, and type **45** in the **Price/Rate** text box as shown in Figure 4.2.

8 Scroll down the window and accept Services as the Income account and then check the **Is taxable** check box, both of which are shown in Figure 4.2.

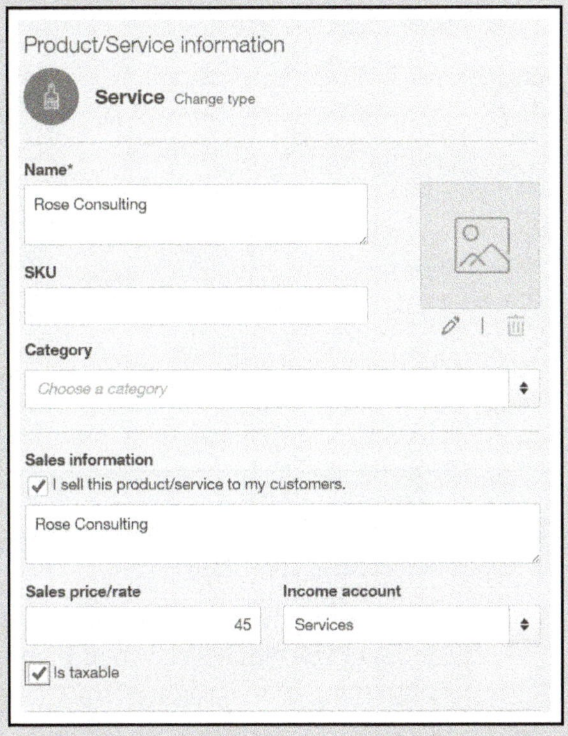

Product/Service information

🞅 **Service** Change type

Name*

Rose Consulting

SKU

Category

Choose a category

Sales information

☑ I sell this product/service to my customers.

Rose Consulting

Sales price/rate   **Income account**

45   Services

☑ Is taxable

Figure 4.2

Product or Service Information (adding a new service)

9   Click on the drop-down arrow to the right of the **Save and Close** button, and select **Save and New**.

10   Click **Change type** and then select **Inventory**.

11   Type **Roses** in the **Name** text box.

12   Type **0** in the **Initial Quantity On Hand** text box and type today's date in the **As Of Date** text box.

13   Select **Inventory Asset** as the Inventory Asset Account.

14   Type **Roses** in the **Sale Information** and in **Purchasing Information** text boxes.

15   Type **25** in the **Price/Rate** text box and **15** in the **Cost** text box.

16   Select **Sales of Product Income** from the Income Account drop-down list and **Cost of Goods Sold** from the Expense Account drop-down list.

17   Check the **Is Taxable** check box. A partial view of the Product or Service Information window should look like Figure 4.3.

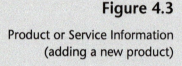

Figure 4.3

Product or Service Information
(adding a new product)

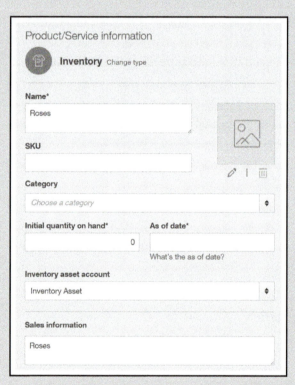

18   Click on the drop-down arrow to the right of the **Save and New** button, and select **Save and Close**.

19   Scroll down the revised list of Products and Service to see the service and product you entered shown in Figure 4.4.

Figure 4.4

Updated List of Products and Services (partial view)

20 Click the **Customers** menu in the Navigation Bar, and click the **New Customer** button.

21 Type **James** in the **First name** text box and **Roxy** in the **Last name** text box.

22 Type **Roxy Corp.** in the Company and in the Display name as text boxes.

23 Select the **Address** tab, and type **101 Ocean View, La Jolla, CA, 92130** in the appropriate text boxes. Click **Save** and then click **Edit** to view the data you just entered. A partial view of the Customer Information window is shown in Figure 4.5.

Figure 4.5

Customer Information window (partial view)

24 Select the **Payment and billing** tab, and select **Net 30** from the Terms text box.

25 Click **Save**.

26 The Roxy Corp. customer window appears shown in Figure 4.6.

Figure 4.6

Roxy Corp. (customer window)

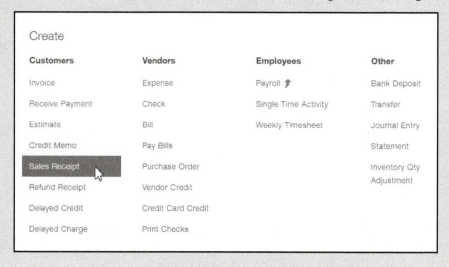

You have now added a new service, a new product, and a new customer. Next up, adding sales receipts to record cash sales and invoices to record credit sales.

Sales Receipts and Invoices

A business uses sales receipts to record sales transactions on a daily basis where payment is received at the same time as a product or service is delivered. Sales invoices are used to record sales transactions where customers are granted credit terms and given some time to pay after a product or service is delivered. In either case, sales are recorded when the product or services are rendered.

To add sales receipts and invoices to the Sample Company, do the following:

1   Continue from where you left off. If you closed the Sample Company, follow the steps to reopen it found at the beginning of this chapter.

2   Click the **Create** (+) icon, and select **Sales Receipt** shown in Figure 4.7.

Figure 4.7

Create window (adding a sales receipt)

3　Select **Bill's Windsurf Shop** from the Choose a customer drop-down list in the upper left corner of the Sales Receipt window.

4　Your computer's system date has been entered as the Sales Receipt date.

5　Select **Check** from the drop-down list of Payment methods.

6　The check will be recorded in the Undeposited Funds account since deposits for this company are made every other day.

7　On line 1 of the sales receipt, select **Pump** from the drop-down list of Products/Services.

8　Type **2** in the QTY (Quantity) column.

9　On line 2 of the sales receipt, select **Rock Fountain** from the drop-down list of Products/Services.

10　Type **2** in the QTY (Quantity) column and then press [**Tab**]. The sales receipt should look like Figure 4.8.

Figure 4.8

Sales Receipt before Sales Tax (partial view)

11　Scroll down the sales receipt, and select **California** from the drop-down list in the **Select a sales tax rate** text box. The lower half of your sales receipt should look like Figure 4.9 with the $46.40 tax amount added.

Figure 4.9

Sales Receipt after Sales Tax (partial view)

12   Click **Save and Close**.

13   Click the **Customers** menu item from the Navigation Bar, and click **Bill's Windsurf Shop**. A listing of recent transactions affecting that customer is shown, including the recorded sales receipt shown in Figure 4.10.

Figure 4.10

Bill's Windsurf Shop (recent transactions)

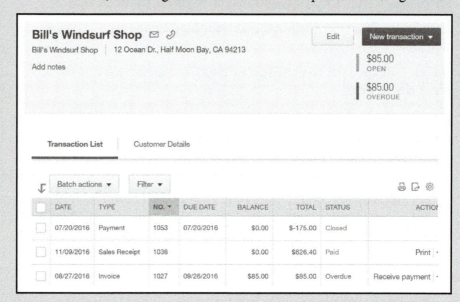

14   Click the **Create (+)** icon, and select **Invoice** shown in Figure 4.11.

Figure 4.11

Create windows (adding an invoice)

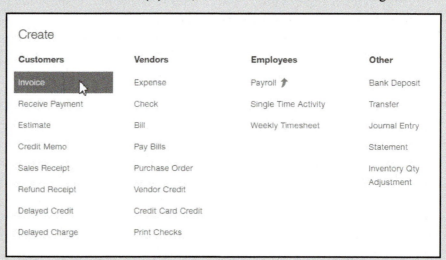

15   Select **Cool Cars** from the Choose a customer drop-down list in the upper left corner of the Invoice window.

16   Your computer's system date has been entered as the Invoice date, and the default terms for this customer are in the appropriate text boxes.

17   On line 1 of the invoice, select **Trimming** from the drop-down list of Products/Services.

18   Type **5** in the Quantity (QTY) column.

19   On line 2 of the sales receipt, select **Pest Control** from the drop-down list of Products/Services.

20 Type **3** in the Quantity (QTY) column and then press [**Tab**]. The invoice should look like Figure 4.12.

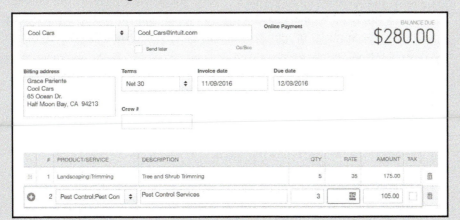

Figure 4.12

Invoice (partial view)

21 Scroll down the invoice and select **California** from the drop-down list in the Select a sales tax rate text box. Even though a rate is selected, no sales tax is applied. Both services are not taxable, and thus, no sales tax is added.

22 Click **Save and Close**.

23 Click the **Customers** menu item from the Navigation Bar and then click **Cool Cars**. A listing of recent transactions affecting that customer is shown, including the recorded invoice shown in Figure 4.13.

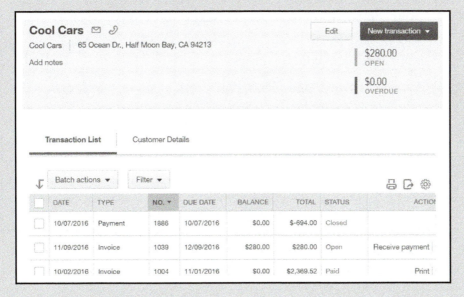

Figure 4.13

Cool Cars (recent transactions)

Cash Receipts

In QBO, the concept of cash receipts is referred to as receiving payments. Thus, to record the receipt of payment from a customer, you can use the Receive Payment item in the **Create (+)** icon to record the transaction, or you can use Receive Payment from the Action column in a customer's list of transactions. Once a payment is received, it must be deposited into your bank account. This is a separate but important process in QBO.

To record the receipt of a payment to the Sample Company from a customer, do the following:

1 Continue from where you left off. If you closed the Sample Company, follow the steps to reopen it found at the beginning of this chapter.

2 Click the **Create (+)** icon, and select **Receive Payment** shown in Figure 4.14.

Figure 4.14

Create window (recording the receipt of a customer payment)

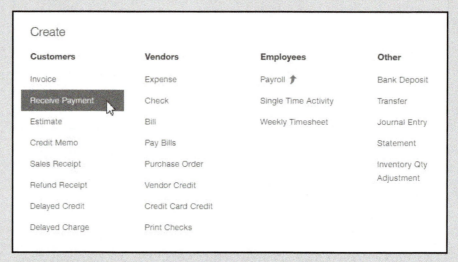

3 Select **Jeff's Jalopies** from the Choose a customer drop-down list in the upper left corner of the Receive Payment window.

4 Your computer's system date has been entered as the Payment date.

5 Select **Check** as the Payment method. The **Undeposited Funds** account will be used to record this check.

6 Place a check in the **Invoice # 1022** check box shown in Figure 4.15 (Do not click Save.)

Figure 4.15

Receive Payment window

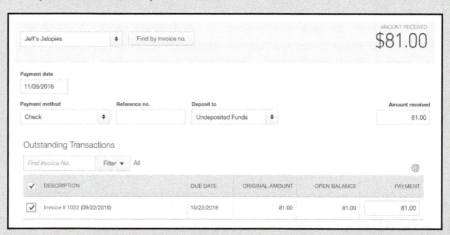

7 Click **Cancel** so you can explore the other means of recording this transaction. Click **Yes** when asked if you want to leave without saving.

8   Click the **Customers** menu item from the Navigation Bar, and click **Jeff's Jalopies**. A listing of recent transactions affecting that customer is shown including invoice # 1022 shown in Figure 4.16.

Figure 4.16

Jeff's Jalopies Recent Transactions

9   Click **Receive payment** in the Action column next to invoice # 1022.

10   The same Receive Payment window you saw earlier reappears. Thus, you have two ways of accessing and recording the receipt of payments from a customer. Enter the same information you did earlier as shown in Figure 4.15, and click **Save and Close**.

11   In the Jeff's Jalopies window, the transactions and payment are shown, and the balance is $0.00 shown in Figure 4.17.

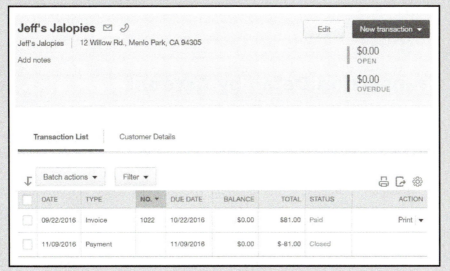

Figure 4.17

Jeff's Jalopies window (recent transactions)

12   Click the **Create (+)** icon, and select **Bank Deposit** from the Other column shown in Figure 4.18.

Figure 4.18

Create window (inputting a bank deposit)

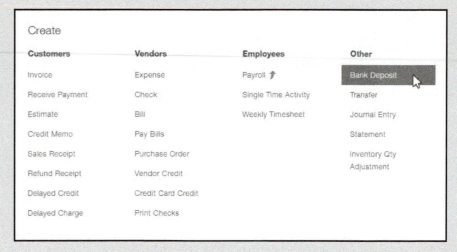

13   Select the payment received from Freeman Sporting Goods from the list of existing payments shown in Figure 4.19.

Figure 4.19

Deposit window

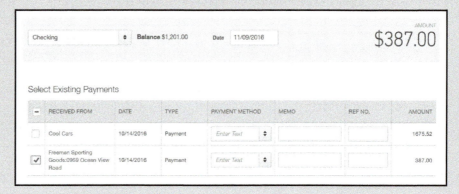

14   Click **Save and Close**.

Transaction Detail by Account

In the cases found at the end of each chapter, you will be asked to create a Trial Balance report as of a certain date. You will compare your Trial Balance report with one provided in the case to see if you have correctly recorded various business events. If your Trial Balance differs, you will need to fix your errors.

A usual explanation for an incorrect Trial Balance report is recording a transaction in an incorrect period, not recording it at all, or recording it incorrectly. To investigate, you will need to create a transaction detail by account report for a specific period. You can create such a report for all transactions to see if yours were recorded in the proper period and to see where you may have entered a wrong amount or account.

To create, print, and export a transaction detail by account report for all transactions, do the following:

1   Continue from your work earlier. (If you do not, none of your work in this chapter will be visible since it is not saved for the Sample Company.)

2   Click **Reports** from the Navigation bar.

3 Type **Transaction** in the Go to Report text box.

4 Select **Transaction Detail by Account**.

5 Select **All Dates** from the Report period drop-down text box.

6 Click **Run Report**. The top of the report is shown in Figure 4.20.

Craig's Design and Landscaping Services

TRANSACTION DETAIL BY ACCOUNT

All Dates

DATE	TRANSACTION TYPE	NUM	NAME	MEMO/DESCRIPTION	SPLIT	AMOUNT	BALANCE
▾ Checking							
05/31/2016	Deposit			Opening Balance	Opening Balance Equity	5,000.00	5,000.00
07/12/2016	Bill Payment (Check)	10	Robertson & Associates		Accounts Payable (A/P)	-300.00	4,700.00
07/20/2016	Payment	1053	Bill's Windsurf Shop		Accounts Receivable (A/R)	175.00	4,875.00
08/03/2016	Expense	12	Robertson & Associates		Legal & Professional Fees:Acco...	-250.00	4,625.00
08/25/2016	Check	4	Chin's Gas and Oil		Automobile:Fuel	-54.55	4,570.45
08/31/2016	Sales Tax Payment			Q1 Payment	-Split-	-38.50	4,531.95
08/31/2016	Sales Tax Payment			Q1 Payment	-Split-	-38.40	4,493.55
09/03/2016	Check	12	Books by Bessie		Legal & Professional Fees:Book...	-55.00	4,438.55

Figure 4.20

Transaction Detail by Account report (top section)

7 Scroll down the report until you locate the deposit you recorded from Freeman Sporting Goods shown in Figure 4.21.

DATE	TRANSACTION TYPE	NUM	NAME	MEMO/DESCRIPTION	SPLIT	AMOUNT	BALANCE
10/13/2016	Bill Payment (Check)	6	PG&E		Accounts Payable (A/P)	-114.09	1,215.25
10/13/2016	Deposit				-Split-	408.00	1,623.25
10/13/2016	Cash Expense		Chin's Gas and Oil		Automobile:Fuel	-63.15	1,560.10
10/14/2016	Expense	76	Pam Seitz		Legal & Professional Fees	-75.00	1,485.10
10/14/2016	Check	75	Hicks Hardware		-Split-	-228.75	1,256.35
10/14/2016	Deposit				-Split-	868.15	2,124.50
10/17/2016	Cash Expense		Tania's Nursery		Job Expenses:Job Materials:Pla...	-23.50	2,101.00
10/28/2016	Credit Card Credit				Mastercard	-900.00	1,201.00
11/09/2016	Deposit		Freeman Sporting Goods:0969 ...		Undeposited Funds	387.00	1,588.00
Total for Checking						$1,588.00	

Figure 4.21

Transaction Detail by Account report (partial view)

8 Click on **Deposit** for Freeman Sporting Goods to view the deposit recorded.

9 Close this window, scroll down the report, and investigate other transactions.

10 Scroll back to the top of this report, and click **Save Customization**.

11 Select **All** from the Share with drop-down list and then click **Save**.

12 Click the **Print** button to set this report up for printing; however, do not print this report since it is too long and unnecessary. Click **Cancel**.

13 Click the **Gear** icon, and click **Sign Out**.

This report can help identifying and correcting errors.

End Note

You have now added a customer, product, and service. You have recorded a sales receipt, invoice, payment received from a customer, and deposit to a bank account. These are operating activities. Additional operating activities related to purchases and cash payments follow in the next chapter.

Chapter 4 Questions

1 What steps need to be followed to add a new product or service?

2 What steps need to be followed to record a new sales receipt?

3 What steps need to be followed to record a new invoice?

4 What steps need to be followed to record a new payment from a customer?

5 What steps need to be followed to record a new deposit to the bank?

6 What are the differences between adding a new product and adding a new service?

7 What is the difference between a sales receipt and a sales invoice?

Chapter 4 Matching

a. Invoice

b. Sales receipt

c. Product

d. Service

e. Create (+) icon

f. Payment from a customer

g. Deposit

h. Pest control

i. Roses

j. Cool Cars

_____ A service in the Sample Company

_____ Providing the bank a payment from a customer

_____ Used when recording a sale on account

_____ Used to access invoices, sales receipts, or bank deposits

_____ A customer in the Sample Company

_____ Quantities of this are not tracked

_____ Used when cash is collected at the time of a sale

_____ Cash receipts received from a sale

_____ Quantities of this are tracked

_____ A product in the Sample Company

Chapter 4 Cases

The following cases require you to open the company you updated in Chapter 3. Each of the following cases continues throughout the text in a sequential manner. For example, if you are assigned Case 01, you will use the file you modified in this chapter in all the following chapters. Each of the following cases is similar in concepts assessed but differs in amounts and transactions.

To reopen your company, do the following:

1 Open your Internet browser.

2 Type **https://qbo.intuit.com/qbo28/loginwebredir** into your browser's address text box.

3 Type your User ID and Password into the text boxes as you have done before.

Case 1

Add some operating activities (sales and cash receipts) to your company.

Based on what you learned in the text and using the Sample Company, you are to add the following transactions to your company:

1 Add a new customer – Name: Sarah Hay, Company: Hey Hays Surf, Display name as: Sarah Hay, Address: 230 Beach Way, La Jolla, CA, 92039.

2 Add a new service – Tune-Up, Rate: $85.00, income account: Services.

3 Add a new product with quantity tracked – Fred Rubble, initial quantity on hand: 0, as of date 1/1/2018, price: $950.00, cost: $600.00, income account: Sales, expense account: Cost of Goods Sold.

4 Record a new sales receipt on 1/3/18 – Customer: Blondie's Boards, payment method: Check, reference no.: 893, deposit to: Undeposited Funds, product: Rook 15, quantity: 2.

5 Record a new invoice on 1/4/18 – Customer: Hey Hays Surf, terms: Net 30, service: Tune-Up, quantity: 2, product: The Water Hog, quantity: 1.

6 Record a new cash payment received on 1/5/18 – Customer: Blondie's Boards, payment method: Check, reference no.: 984, deposit to: Undeposited Funds, amount received: $5,000.00.

7 Record a deposit made on 1/8/18 to the checking account – Received from: Blondie's Boards, amount received: $1,300.00, related to: Sales Receipt.

8 Prepare a Trial Balance report with a From date of 1/1/18 and a To date of 1/31/18, save it as a customized report named Trial Balance 1/31/18, and share it with all users. Your report should look like Figure 4.22. If asked, indicate that your business is accrual based.

Figure 4.22

Trial Balance (as of 1/31/18)

Case 1
TRIAL BALANCE
As of January 31, 2018

	DEBIT	CREDIT
Checking	26,300.00	
Accounts Receivable	1,030.00	
Inventory Asset	6,700.00	
Prepaid Expenses	3,000.00	
Undeposited Funds	5,000.00	
Furniture & Fixtures:Depreciation		10,000.00
Furniture & Fixtures:Original cost	40,000.00	
Accounts Payable		4,500.00
Notes Payable		60,000.00
Common Stock		1,000.00
Opening Balance Equity		0.00
Retained Earnings		5,500.00
Sales		2,160.00
Services		170.00
Cost of Goods Sold	1,300.00	
TOTAL	$83,330.00	$83,330.00

9 If your trial balance differs from what is in Figure 4.22, do the following:

a. Make sure that all of your changes were dated in January 2018.

b. Click on the debit or credit balance to view a transactions report for each account, and investigate why your answer differs.

c. Ask your instructor for assistance.

d. Be sure your company matches the above since, in the following chapter, you will add additional business events.

10 Export your Trial Balance report to Excel, and save it with the file name: Student Name (replace with your name) Ch 04 Case 01 Trial Balance.xlsx.

11 Open and print the custom report you created in the last chapter called Transaction Detail by Account.

12 Use your Transaction Detail by Account report to locate any differences in your Trial Balance report created above.

a. Make sure all of your changes were dated in January 2018.

b. Click on the line that does not match to view the transaction for that account, and investigate why your answer differs.

c. Ask your instructor for assistance.

d. Be sure your company matches the above since, in the following chapter, you will add additional business events.

13 Export your Transactions Detail by Account report to Excel and save it with the file name: Student Name (replace with your name) Ch 04 Case 01 Transaction Detail by Account.xlsx.

14 Sign out of your company.

Case 2

Add some operating activities (sales and cash receipts) to your company. Based on what you learned in the text and using the Sample Company, you are to add the following transactions:

1 Add a new customer – Hagen's Toys, 3983 Torrey Pines, La Jolla, CA, 92039.

2 Add a new service – Custom Painting, Rate: $45.00, income account: Services.

3 Add 2 new products with quantity tracked – GO Aircraft Radio, initial quantity on hand: 0, as of date 1/1/2019, price: $4,999.00, cost: $2,500.00, income account: Sales, expense account: Cost of Goods Sold and Taylor 22cc, initial quantity on hand: 0, as of date 1/1/2019, price: $2,999.00, cost: $1,500.00, income account: Sales, expense account: Cost of Goods Sold.

4 Record a new sales receipt on 1/3/19 – Customer: Benson's RC, payment method: Credit Card, reference no.: 16756, deposit to: Undeposited Funds, product: Broon F830 Ride, quantity: 3.

5 Record a new invoice on 1/4/19 – Customer: Hagen's Toys, terms: Net 30, service: Custom Painting, quantity: 5, product: Seawind Carbon Sailboat, quantity: 1.

6 Record a new cash payment received on 1/7/19 – Customer: Benson's RC, payment method: Check, reference no.: 9847, deposit to: Undeposited Funds, amount received: $925.00.

7 Record a deposit made on 1/7/19 to the checking account – Received from: Benson's RC, amount received: $4,500.00, related to: Sales Receipt.

8 Prepare a Trial Balance report with a From date of 1/1/19 and a To date of 1/31/19, save it as a customized report named Trial Balance 1/31/19, and share it with all users. Your report should look like Figure 4.23. If asked, indicate that your business is accrual based.

Figure 4.23

Trial Balance (as of 1/31/19)

Case 2
TRIAL BALANCE
As of January 31, 2019

	DEBIT	CREDIT
Checking	9,500.00	
Accounts Receivable	1,425.00	
Inventory Asset	2,040.00	
Prepaid Expenses	2,400.00	
Undeposited Funds	925.00	
Machinery & Equipment:Depreciation		1,000.00
Machinery & Equipment:Original cost	10,000.00	
Accounts Payable		1,900.00
Notes Payable		12,000.00
Common Stock		100.00
Opening Balance Equity		0.00
Retained Earnings		8,385.00
Sales		5,700.00
Services		225.00
Cost of Goods Sold	3,020.00	
TOTAL	$29,310.00	$29,310.00

9   If your trial balance differs from what is in Figure 4.23, do the following:

   a.   Make sure that all of your changes were dated in January 2019.

   b.   Click on the debit or credit balance to view a transactions report for each account, and investigate why your answer differs.

   c.   Ask your instructor for assistance.

   d.   Be sure your company matches the above since, in the following chapter, you will add additional business events.

10   Export your Trial Balance report to Excel and save it with the file name: Student Name (replace with your name) Ch 04 Case 02 Trial Balance. xlsx.

11   Open and print the custom report you created in the last chapter called Transaction Detail by Account.

12   Use your Transaction Detail by Account report to locate any differences in your Trial Balance report created above.

   a.   Make sure that all of your changes were dated in January 2019.

   b.   Click on the line that does not match to view the transaction for that account, and investigate why your answer differs.

   c.   Ask your instructor for assistance.

   d.   Be sure your company matches the above since, in the following chapter, you will add additional business events.

13 Export your Transactions Detail by Account report to Excel and save it with the file name: Student Name (replace with your name) Ch 04 Case 02 Transaction Detail by Account.xlsx.

14 Sign out of your company.

Case 3

Now it's time for you to add some operating activities (sales and cash receipts) to your company.

Based on what you have learned in the text, using the Sample Company, you are to add the following transactions:

1 Add a new customer – Surfer Sales, 3983 Torrey Pines, La Jolla, CA, 92039.

2 Add a new service – Phone Consulting, Rate: $35.00, income account: Services, not taxable.

3 Add two new products – Apple iPhone 6s, initial quantity on hand: 0, Inventory asset account: Inventory Asset, price: $549.00, cost: $349.00, income account: Sales of Product Income, expense account: Cost of Goods Sold, taxable and Apple iPhone 7 Plus, initial quantity on hand: 0, Inventory asset account: Inventory Asset, price: $800, cost: $600.00, income account: Sales of Product Income expense account: Cost of Goods Sold, taxable. (Use your current system date as the "as of date" for both products.)

4 Record a new sales receipt on 1/3/20 – customer: Surfer Sales, payment method: Credit Card, reference no.: 16756, deposit to: Undeposited Funds, product: Apple iPhone 7, quantity: 6, and 3 hours of Phone Consulting. Be sure to select California from the **Select a sales tax** drop-down list in the sales receipt window.

5 Record a new invoice on 1/6/20 – customer: GHO Marketing, terms: Net 30, 3 hours of Apple Repairs, product: iPhone 7, quantity: 3. Be sure to select California from the **Select a sales tax** drop-down list in the sales receipt window.

6 Record a new cash payment received on select California from the Select a sales tax drop-down list in the sales receipt window. 1/7/20 – customer: GHO Marketing, payment method: Check, reference no.: 9847, deposit to: Undeposited Funds, amount received: $4,125.00.

7 Record a deposit made on 1/9/20 to the checking account of $9,180.00 which was received from: Surfer Sales, amount $5,055.00, related to: Sales Receipt and GHO Marketing, amount $4,125.00, related to: Payment.

8 Prepare a Trial Balance report with a From date of 1/1/20 and a To date of 1/31/20 and then save it as a customized report named Trial Balance 1/31/20 and share it with all users. Your report should look like Figure 4.24.

Figure 4.24

Trial Balance as of 1/31/20

Case 3 - Student Name (ID number)

TRIAL BALANCE

As of January 31, 2020

	DEBIT	CREDIT
Checking	21,180.00	
Accounts Receivable (A/R)	2,610.00	
Inventory Asset	1,700.00	
Prepaid Expenses	2,750.00	
Undeposited Funds	0.00	
Machinery & Equipment:Depreciation		2,000.00
Machinery & Equipment:Original cost	15,000.00	
Accounts Payable (A/P)		5,000.00
State Board of Equalization Payable		675.00
Notes Payable		23,000.00
Opening Balance Equity		0.00
Owner's Equity		10,075.00
Sales of Product Income		6,750.00
Services		240.00
Cost of Goods Sold	4,500.00	
TOTAL	**$47,740.00**	**$47,740.00**

9 If your trial balance is different than Figure 4.24:

   a. Make sure that all of your changes were dated in January 2020.

   b. Click on the debit or credit balance to view a transactions report for each account and investigate why your answer is different.

   c. Ask your instructor for assistance.

   d. Be sure your company matches the above, as in the following chapter you'll be adding additional business events.

10 Export your Trial Balance report to Excel and save it with the file name: Student Name (replace with your name) Ch 04 Case 03 Trial Balance. xlsx.

11 Open and print the custom report you created in the last chapter called Transaction Detail by Account.

12 Use your Transaction Detail by Account report to locate any differences in your Trial Balance report created above.

   a. Make sure that all of your changes were dated January 2020.

   b. Click on the line that doesn't match to view the transaction for that account and investigate why your answer is different.

    c. Ask your instructor for assistance.

    d. Be sure your company matches the above, as in the following chapter you'll be adding additional business events.

13 Export your Transactions Detail by Account report to Excel and save it with the file name: Student Name (replace with your name) Ch 04 Case 03 Transaction Detail by Account.xlsx.

14 Sign out of your company.

5

Operating Activities: Purchases and Cash Payments

Student Learning Outcomes

Upon completion of this chapter, the student will be able to do the following:

- Create a vendor
- Record a purchase order
- Record a bill for the receipt of products/services on account
- Record the payment of bills
- Record credit card charges
- Record checks
- Prepare a Trial Balance and drill down to a transaction report for an account

Overview

Intuit has provided a sample company online to provide new users a test drive of its QBO product. In this chapter, you will open this sample company and practice various features of QBO. You will be recording operating activities, such as adding vendors, purchase orders, bills, bill payments, credit card charges, and checks to the Sample Company file. Remember, if you stop in the middle of this work, none of your work will be saved. So, when you return, the same Sample Company, without your work, will appear. In the end of chapter work, you will be asked to perform the same tasks completed on the Sample Company on your Student Company. That work, of course, will be saved.

Vendors

In this section you will be adding new vendors. Recall that vendors are your company's suppliers of products and services. To add vendors you will use the Vendors menu item in the Navigation Bar.

To add new vendors to the Sample Company, do the following:

1 Open your Internet browser.

2 Type **https://qbo.intuit.com/redir/testdrive** into your browser's address text box, and then press [**Enter**] to view the Sample Company Home page.

3 Click the **Vendors** menu in the Navigation Bar, and click the **New Vendor** button.

4   Type **Valley Rock** in the Company and Display name text boxes.

5   Type the address **290 Central Ave., Middletown, CA, 94482** in the appropriate text boxes.

6   Select **Net 30** from the Terms text box. A Vendor Information window is shown in Figure 5.1

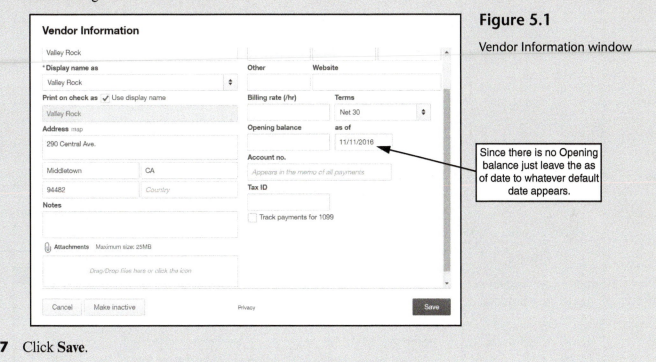

Figure 5.1

Vendor Information window

Vendor Information

Valley Rock

*Display name as
Valley Rock

Print on check as ✓ Use display name
Valley Rock

Address map
290 Central Ave.

Middletown   CA

94482   *Country*

Notes

📎 **Attachments** Maximum size: 25MB

Drag/Drop files here or click the icon

Other   Website

Billing rate (/hr)   Terms
                             Net 30

Opening balance   as of
                             11/11/2016

Account no.
Appears in the memo of all payments

Tax ID

☐ Track payments for 1099

Since there is no Opening balance just leave the as of date to whatever default date appears.

Cancel   Make inactive   Privacy   Save

7   Click **Save**.

You have added a new vendor. Next up, adding purchase orders.

Purchase Orders

A business uses purchase orders to formally order products or services from its vendors. Purchase orders are also used as a reference and control for products received. During the creation of a purchase order, you can create a new product. Purchase orders can be for inventory or for products ordered for a specific customer.

To add two purchase orders and new product to the Sample Company, do the following:

1   Continue from where you left off above.

2   Click the **Create** (+) icon, and select **Purchase Order** as shown in Figure 5.2.

Figure 5.2

Create windows (adding a
purchase order)

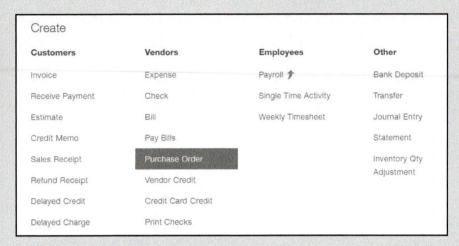

3   Select **Valley Rock** from the Choose a vendor drop-down list in the upper
left corner of the Purchase Order window.

4   Your computer's system date has been entered as the purchase order date.

5   Click in the **Product/Service** column on line 1 of the purchase order's
Item details section, and select **Add New** shown in Figure 5.3.

Figure 5.3

Purchase Order (adding a
new product)

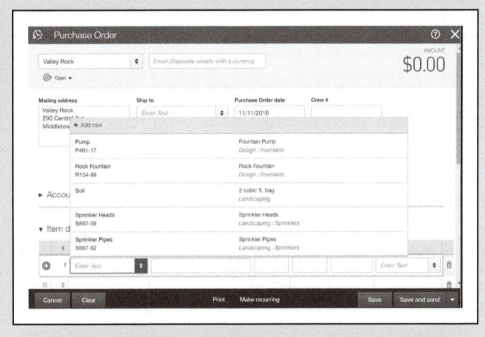

6   Create a new product, as you have done before – product type: **Inventory**,
name and description: **Landscape Rock**, initial quantity on hand: **0**,
inventory asset account: **Inventory Asset**, Sales price: **75**, cost: **50**, income
account: **Sales of Product Income**, expense account: **Cost of Goods Sold**,
is taxable: **yes**. Click **Save and Close**.

7 Type **100** in the Quantity (QTY) column. Leave the Customer field blank as this order is for inventory. Your completed purchase order should look like Figure 5.4.

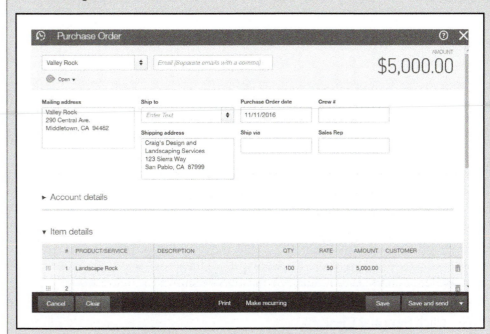

Figure 5.4

Purchase Order (for Valley Rock)

8 Click **Save and New**.

9 Select **Hicks Hardware** from the Choose a vendor drop-down list in the upper left corner of the Purchase Order window. Accept your current system date as the purchase order date.

10 The Item details section of the purchase order is filled out with information from the last purchase order completed for this vendor. Leave all lines of the Product/Service column as it is.

11 Change the amounts in the Quantity (QTY) column as follows: Rock Fountain **3**, Sprinkler Heads **20**, Sprinkler Pipes **30**, and Pump **4**.

12 Select **Kookies by Kathy** in the Customer column for all four items so your purchase order looks like Figure 5.5.

Figure 5.5

Purchase Order (to Hicks Hardware)

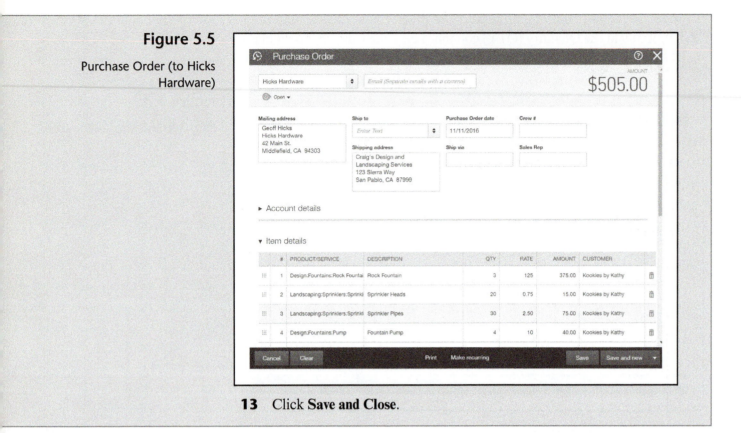

13 Click **Save and Close**.

Bills

In the previous chapter, you created invoices to customers for products or services rendered. That invoice served as a bill to that customer signifying a sales transaction for you and a bill to them. Likewise, when you enter into a business transaction, such as purchasing a product or service from a vendor, you expect them to send you an invoice. In QBO, the invoice you receive from a vendor is called a bill. Bills are recorded in QBO to signify the receipt of a product or service and a related liability, usually accounts payable. The inventory account is affected when the bill represents a product being delivered.

In QBO, the terms of those bills could be one of the following: due on receipt, net 10, net 15, net 30, or net 60. The net reference means the bill is due to be paid within a specified number of days, for example, 10, 15, 30, or 60 days. Other terms, for example, 2/10 net 30, provide for a 2% discount on the invoice if paid within 10 days; otherwise, a payment is required within 30 days. Even though you can set up such terms to appear on invoices to customers and bills from vendors, QBO does not calculate them automatically. To simplify your learning of QBO, discounts have not been implemented in this text.

In this section, you will focus on recording a bill for the receipt of services and products on account, meaning you will have been given terms (usually net 30), so you will not have to pay the bill for 30 days after the bill date. The first product purchased had been previously ordered using a purchase order. The second product ordered is a new product, which had not been previously ordered using a purchase order. Both of these purchases will affect inventory and are, thus, recorded in the Items detail section of a bill. The third transaction is a service that was rendered and does not affect inventory and is, therefore, recorded in the Accounts detail section of a bill.

To record a bill from a vendor for the receipt of products/services on account, do the following:

1 Continue from where you left off.

2 Click the **Create (+)** icon, and click **Bill** in the Vendor column shown in Figure 5.6.

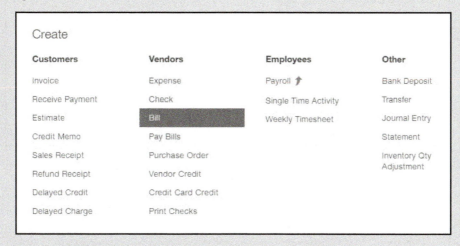

Figure 5.6

Create window (entering bills)

3 Select **Tim Phillip Masonry** from the Choose a vendor drop-down list.

4 Select **Net 30** from the drop-down list of terms. Accept your current system date as the Bill date.

5 Collapse the Account details section of the bill by clicking on the arrow next to **Account details.**

6 Expand the Item details section of the bill by clicking on the arrow next to **Item details.**

7 Click **Add All** in the Add to Bill section, which identifies an open purchase order #1002 from this vendor located on the right of the bill shown in Figure 5.7.

Figure 5.7

Bill (adding purchase order information)

8   Collapse the Account details section of the bill by clicking on the arrow next to **Account details.**

9   The purchase order contains information from purchase order #1002 shown in Figure 5.8.

Figure 5.8

Bill (after purchase order information is added)

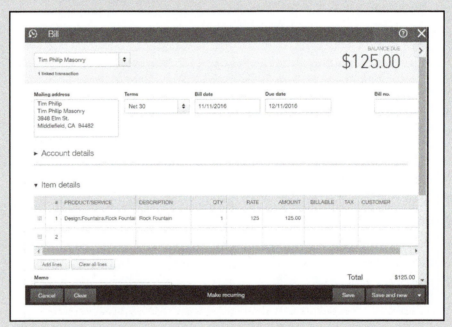

10   Click **Save and New**.

11   Select **Tania's Nursery** from the Choose a vendor drop-down list.

12   Select **Net 30** from the drop-down list of terms. Accept your current system date as the Bill date.

13   Select **Add new** on line 1 of the bill in the Product/Service column.

14   Add a new product as you have done before – product type: **Inventory**, name, and description: **Lavender**, initial quantity on hand: **0**, inventory

asset account: **Inventory Asset**, Sales price: **15**, cost: **10**, income account: **Sales of Product Income**, expense account: **Cost of Goods Sold**, is taxable: **yes**. Click **Save and Close** in the Product/Service Information window.

15   Select **Lavender** in the Product/Service column of the Item details section of the bill and then type **100** on line 1 of the bill in the Quantity (QTY) column.

16   Click **Save and New.**

17   Select **Computers by Jenni** from the Choose a vendor drop-down list.

18   Select **Net 30** from the drop-down list of terms. Accept your current system date as the Bill date.

19   Expand the Account details section of the bill by clicking on the **arrow next to Account details.**

20   Collapse the Item details section of the bill by clicking on the **arrow next to Item details.**

21   Select **Equipment Rental** on line 1 of the bill in the Account column.

22   Type **1,200** on line 1 of the bill in the Amount column shown in Figure 5.9.

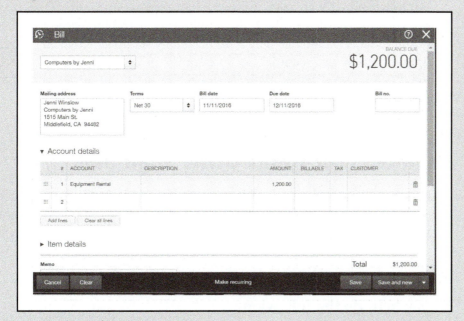

Figure 5.9

Bill (for services)

23   Click **Save and New.**

24   Select **Brosnahan Insurance Agency** from the Choose a vendor drop-down list.

25   Accept **Net 10** from the drop-down list of terms.

26   The bill information is filled in automatically based on the last bill entered for this vendor.

27   Select **Prepaid Expenses** on line 1 of the bill in the Account column replacing Insurance.

28   Type **1,800** on line 1 of the bill in the Amount column replacing the existing amount shown in Figure 5.10.

Figure 5.10

Bill for Prepaid Expenses (recording)

29   Click **Save and Close**. Close the Bill window.

All bills entered increased an asset or an expense account. Inventory purchases were all recorded in the Item details section and increased the quantity of those products (as long as they were originally set up as "tracked" products). Equipment rental was recorded as an expense and the prepaid insurance was recorded as an asset (Prepaid Expenses). All bills increased the accounts payable liability account.

Payment of Bills, Use of a Credit Card, Payments for Items Other than Bills

In this section, you will focus on recording the payment of a bill for the receipt of services and/or products on account, recording credit card charges, or recording the payment by check for other items.

To pay bills, do the following:

1   Continue from where you left off.

2   Click the **Create** (+) icon, and click **Pay Bills** in the Vendor column shown in Figure 5.11.

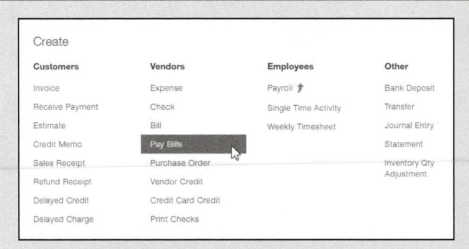

Figure 5.11

Create window (paying bills)

3 A listing of possible bills that can be paid appears. In the Pay Bills window, select **Checking** from the drop-down list in the Payment Account box shown in Figure 5.12.

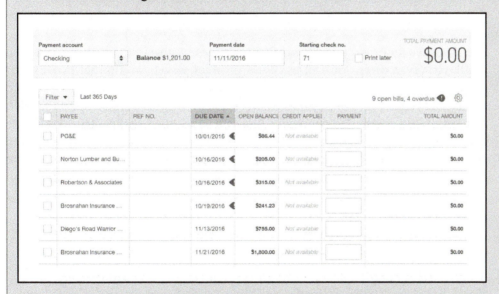

Figure 5.12

Bills to Pay

4 Click and hold your mouse between the PAYEE and REF NO. columns and drag to the right to increase the width of the PAYEE column.

5 Click and hold your mouse between the REF NO. and DUE DATE columns and drag to the left to decrease the width of the REF NO. column.

6 Click in the check box of payees PG&E, Norton Lumber and Building Materials, Robertson & Associates, and Brosnahan Insurance Agency shown in Figure 5.13.

Figure 5.13

Bills to Pay (selecting)

7   Click **Save and Close**.

You have now paid bills for products/services received for which you received a bill. However, often you will pay for a product/service or another expense for which you have not received a bill. Often, these are vendors, who give you no terms, and require you to pay immediately. These terms are called *due on receipt*. For example, a credit card charge for fuel or a check for supplies. To record these transactions, you will use either the Expense task or the Check task after clicking the Create (+) icon. For ease of use, you will be directed to use the Expense task for all credit card transactions and the Check task for all checking account payments even though the Expense task can be used for either credit card charges or check payments.

To record a credit card or check payment, do the following:

1   Click the **Create** (+) icon.

2   Click **Expense** under the Vendor column.

3   Select **Chin's Gas and Oil** from the drop-down list in the Choose a payee text box.

4   Select **Mastercard** from the drop-down list in the Choose an account text box.

5   Accept **Automobile:Fuel** in the row 1 Account column and then type **85.00** as the amount replacing the existing 52.56 shown in Figure 5.14.

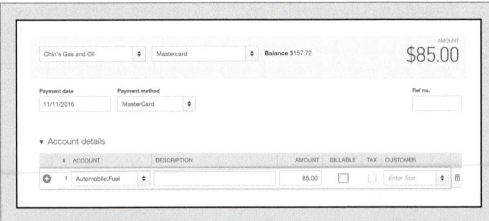

Figure 5.14

Credit Card Charge

6 Click **Save and Close.**

7 Click the **Create** (+) icon.

8 Click **Check** under the Vendor column.

9 Select **Cal Telephone** from the drop-down list in the **Choose a payee** text box.

10 Select **Checking** from the drop-down list in the **Choose an account** text box (it should be selected).

11 Type **77** in the **Check no.** text box.

12 Type **Utilities:Telephone** in the row 1 Account column, and type **325.00** as the amount shown in Figure 5.15.

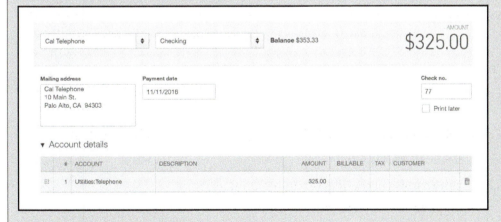

Figure 5.15

Check #77 (payment)

13 Click **Save and Close.**

Trial Balance

The work you completed in this chapter had an effect on the company's trial balance. You decided to create a Trial Balance report and investigate the checking, inventory asset, and accounts payable accounts. In the process, you realized that purchase orders do not affect a company's accounts until products are received or services are rendered.

Trouble? Recall the previous discussion of dates and amounts when using the Sample company. Dates in the text figures will be different than what you see in QBO when using the Sample company. Ending balances may also be different as they will all depend on what actual date you are entering transactions. Focus on the process rather than the resulting report dates or balances. This will not be the situation when you work on the end-of-chapter cases as those dates have been specifically identified.

To create a trial balance and investigate some account activity, do the following:

1   Click **Reports,** type **Trial Balance** into the Go to report text box, and press [**Enter**]. The upper portion of that report is shown in Figure 5.16.

Figure 5.16

Trial Balance (upper portion)

Craig's Design and Landscaping Services

TRIAL BALANCE

As of November 11, 2016

	DEBIT	CREDIT
Checking	28.33	
Savings	800.00	
Accounts Receivable (A/R)	5,281.52	
Inventory Asset	1,721.25	
Prepaid Expenses	1,800.00	
Undeposited Funds	2,062.52	
Truck:Original Cost	13,495.00	
Accounts Payable (A/P)		4,880.00
Mastercard		242.72
Arizona Dept. of Revenue Payable		0.00
Board of Equalization Payable		370.94
Loan Payable		4,000.00
Notes Payable		25,000.00

2   Click the Checking account balance of **28.33** to produce a Transaction Report for the Checking Account. The four bill payment checks you recorded earlier in this chapter and the check payment to Cal Telephone are shown in Figure 5.17.

Craig's Design and Landscaping Services

TRANSACTION REPORT

November 1-11, 2016

DATE	TRANSACTION TYPE	NUM	NAME	MEMO/DESCRIPTION	ACCOUNT	SPLIT	AMOUNT	BALANCE
▾ Checking								
Beginning Balance								1,201.00
11/11/2016	Check	77	Cal Telephone		Checking	Utilities:Telephone	-325.00	876.00
11/11/2016	Bill Payment (Check)	74	Brosnahan Insurance Agency	7653412	Checking	Accounts Payable (A/P)	-241.23	634.77
11/11/2016	Bill Payment (Check)	71	PG&E	00649587213	Checking	Accounts Payable (A/P)	-86.44	548.33
11/11/2016	Bill Payment (Check)	72	Norton Lumber and Building Ma...	32980256	Checking	Accounts Payable (A/P)	-205.00	343.33
11/11/2016	Bill Payment (Check)	73	Robertson & Associates	000005641	Checking	Accounts Payable (A/P)	-315.00	28.33
Total for Checking							**$ -1,172.67**	
TOTAL							**$ -1,172.67**	

Figure 5.17

Transaction Report (for the checking account)

3 Click **Print** to print this report.

4 Click **Back to report summary.**

5 Click the Inventory Asset account balance of **1,721.25** to produce a Transaction Report for the Inventory Asset account. The two bills for product purchases you recorded earlier in this chapter are shown in Figure 5.18.

Craig's Design and Landscaping Services

TRANSACTION REPORT

November 1-11, 2016

DATE	TRANSACTION TYPE	NUM	NAME	MEMO/DESCRIPTION	ACCOUNT	SPLIT	AMOUNT	BALANCE
▾ Inventory Asset								
Beginning Balance								596.25
11/11/2016	Bill		Tania's Nursery	Lavender	Inventory Asset	Accounts Payable (A/P)	1,000.00	1,596.25
11/11/2016	Inventory Starting Value	START		Landscape Rock - Opening inve...	Inventory Asset	Opening Balance Equity	0.00	1,596.25
11/11/2016	Inventory Starting Value	START		Lavender - Opening inventory an...	Inventory Asset	Opening Balance Equity	0.00	1,596.25
11/11/2016	Bill		Tim Philip Masonry	Rock Fountain	Inventory Asset	Accounts Payable (A/P)	125.00	1,721.25
Total for Inventory Asset							**$1,125.00**	
TOTAL							**$1,125.00**	

Figure 5.18

Transaction Report (for the Inventory Asset Account)

6 Click **Print** to print this report.

7 Click **Back to report summary.**

8 Click the Accounts Payable (A/P) account balance of **4,880.00** to produce a Transaction Report for the Accounts Payable (A/P) account. The bills for product and service purchases and the bill payments you recorded earlier in this chapter are shown in Figure 5.19.

Craig's Design and Landscaping Services

TRANSACTION REPORT

November 1-11, 2016

DATE	TRANSACTION TYPE	NUM	NAME	MEMO/DESCRIPTION	ACCOUNT	SPLIT	AMOUNT	BALANCE
▾ Accounts Payable (A/P)								
Beginning Balance								1,602.67
11/11/2016	Bill		Tim Philip Masonry		Accounts Payable (A/P)	Inventory Asset	125.00	1,727.67
11/11/2016	Bill		Tania's Nursery		Accounts Payable (A/P)	Inventory Asset	1,000.00	2,727.67
11/11/2016	Bill		Computers by Jenni		Accounts Payable (A/P)	Equipment Rental	1,200.00	3,927.67
11/11/2016	Bill Payment (Check)	74	Brosnahan Insurance Agency		Accounts Payable (A/P)	Checking	-241.23	3,686.44
11/11/2016	Bill Payment (Check)	71	PG&E		Accounts Payable (A/P)	Checking	-86.44	3,600.00
11/11/2016	Bill Payment (Check)	72	Norton Lumber and Building Mat...		Accounts Payable (A/P)	Checking	-205.00	3,395.00
11/11/2016	Bill Payment (Check)	73	Robertson & Associates		Accounts Payable (A/P)	Checking	-315.00	3,080.00
11/11/2016	Bill		Brosnahan Insurance Agency		Accounts Payable (A/P)	Prepaid Expenses	1,800.00	4,880.00
Total for Accounts Payable (A/P)							**$3,277.33**	
TOTAL							**$3,277.33**	

Figure 5.19

Transaction Report (for the Accounts Payable account)

9 Click **Print** to print this report.

10 Click **Back to Summary Report.**

11 Click the Gear icon, and click **Sign Out.**

End Note

In this chapter, you added a vendor, a product, purchase orders, bills, payment of bills, a credit card purchase, and a check payment. You also produced a trial balance and drilled down through that trial balance to see the effect the bills and payment of bills affected accounts. In the next chapter, you will work with investing and financing activities.

Chapter 5 Questions

1 Why does a business use purchase orders?

2 Describe the steps to create a new product from within a purchase order.

3 What happens when you create a new purchase order to a vendor from whom you recently placed a different purchase order?

4 What accounts are affected when a bill from a vendor supplying you products is recorded?

5 What appears when you click Pay Bills after clicking the Create (+) icon?

6 Describe the process for increasing or decreasing the width of a column in the listing of bills to pay.

7 What are the steps to record a credit card charge?

8 What are the steps to record a check written to pay something other than bills?

9 What are the steps to view a transaction report for the checking account from a trial balance?

10 What are the steps to view a transaction report for the inventory account from a trial balance?

Chapter 5 Matching

a. Purchase order

b. Due on receipt

c. Bill

d. Net 30

e. Item detail section

f. Account detail section

g. Pay Bills

h. Check

i. Expense

j. Vendor

_____ Purchases that affect inventory are recorded here

_____ An invoice sent by a vendor to a customer

_____ Purchases that don't affect inventory are recorded here

_____ Task used to record checks in the checking account

_____ Suppliers of products and services

_____ A formal means to order products from vendors

_____ Pay a bill within 30 days after the bill date

_____ Task used to record credit card charges

_____ Terms that provide no credit

_____ Paying vendors who have billed you

Chapter 5 Cases

The following cases require you to open the company you updated in Chapter 4. Each of the following cases continues throughout the text in a sequential manner. For example, if you are assigned Case 01, you will use the file you modified in this chapter in all following chapters. Each of the following cases is similar in concepts assessed but differs in amounts and transactions.

To reopen your company, do the following:

1   Open your Internet browser.

2   Type **https://qbo.intuit.com/qbo28/loginwebredir** into your browser's address text box.

3   Type your User ID and Password into the text boxes as you have done before.

Case 1

Add some operating activities (purchases, credit card charges, and cash payments) to your company.

Based on what you learned in the text and using the Sample Company, you will add the following transactions to your company:

1   Add a new vendor – Stewart Surfboards, 2102 S El Camino Real, San Clemente, CA 92672 terms: net 30.

2   Add a new vendor – Village Travel, 100 S El Camino Real, San Clemente, CA 92672 terms: due on receipt.

3   Add a new vendor – Office Depot, 101 Main St., San Diego, CA 92600 terms: due on receipt.

4   Add a new account – Category type: Credit Card, detail type: Credit Card, name: VISA.

5   Add a new account – Category type: Other Current Assets, detail type: Other Current Assets, name: Supplies Asset.

6   Add a new tracked product – Name/description: California Nose Rider, initial quantity on hand: 0, inventory asset account: Inventory Asset, price: 3,200.00, cost: 1,700.00, income account: Sales, expense account: Cost of Goods Sold.

7   Add a new tracked product – Name/description: 808, initial quantity on hand: 0, inventory asset account: Inventory Asset, price: 2,700.00, cost: 1,500.00, income account: Sales, expense account: Cost of Goods Sold.

8   Record a new purchase order for products on 1/2/18 – Vendor: Channel Islands, product 1: Fred Rubble, QTY: 5, product 2: Rook 15, QTY: 4, product 3: The Water Hog, QTY: 1.

9   Record a new purchase order for products on 1/3/18 – Vendor: Stewart Surfboards, product 1: 808, QTY: 2, product 2: California Nose Rider, QTY: 1.

10   Record a new bill based on a purchase order #1001 on 1/5/18 – Vendor: Channel Islands, terms: Net 15. All items ordered were received.

11   Record a new bill without a purchase order on 1/8/18 – New vendor: San Diego Gas & Electric, terms: Net 15, account: Utilities, amount: 145.00.

12 Record a new bill without a purchase order on 1/9/18 – New vendor: Prime Properties, terms: Net 15, account 1: Rent or Lease, amount: 2,500.00, account 2: Prepaid Expenses, amount: 5,000.00.

13 Pay all bills due to Channel Islands on 1/19/18 using the checking account and starting with check no. 1001.

14 Record a credit card charge on 1/10/18, vendor: Village Travel, using credit card: VISA, account: Travel, amount: 1,800.00.

15 Record check on 1/11/18, no.: 1002, vendor: Office Depot, amount: 375.00, account: Supplies Asset.

16 Open your previously customized report named Trial Balance 1/31/18. If a cash or accrual message appears just close the message. Your report should look like Figure 5.20.

Case 1
TRIAL BALANCE
As of January 31, 2018

	DEBIT	CREDIT
Checking	16,325.00	
Accounts Receivable	1,030.00	
Inventory Asset	11,800.00	
Prepaid Expenses	8,000.00	
Supplies Asset	375.00	
Undeposited Funds	5,000.00	
Furniture & Fixtures:Depreciation		10,000.00
Furniture & Fixtures:Original cost	40,000.00	
Accounts Payable		7,645.00
VISA		1,800.00
Notes Payable		60,000.00
Common Stock		1,000.00
Opening Balance Equity		0.00
Retained Earnings		5,500.00
Sales		2,160.00
Services		170.00
Cost of Goods Sold	1,300.00	
Rent or Lease	2,500.00	
Travel	1,800.00	
Utilities	145.00	
TOTAL	$88,275.00	$88,275.00

Figure 5.20

Trial Balance (as of 1/31/18)

17 Create and print a Transaction Report for the Checking account as you did earlier in the chapter.

18 Create and print a Transaction Report for the Inventory Asset account as you did earlier in the chapter.

19 Create and print a Transaction Report for the Accounts Payable (A/P) account as you did earlier in the chapter.

20 If your trial balance differs from what is in Figure 5.20, do the following:

a. Make sure all of your changes were dated in January 2018.

b. View the Transaction Reports you just created to locate any errors.

c. Ask your instructor for assistance.

d. Be sure your company matches the above, as in the following chapter you'll be adding additional business events.

21 Export your Trial Balance report to Excel and save it with the file name: Student Name (replace with your name) Ch 05 Case 01 Trial Balance.xlsx.

22 Open and print the custom report you created in the last chapter called Transaction Detail by Account.

23 Export your Transactions Detail by Account report to Excel and save it with the file name: Student Name (replace with your name) Ch 05 Case 01 Transaction Detail by Account.xlsx.

24 Sign out of your company.

Case 2

Add some operating activities (purchases, credit card charges, and cash payments) to your company.

Based on what you learned in the text and using the Sample Company, you will add the following transactions to your company:

1 Add a new vendor – E-flite, 700 Annapolis Ln N Suite #175, Plymouth, MN, 55447, terms: net 15.

2 Add a new vendor – Village Steak House, 100 S El Camino Real, San Clemente, CA 92672 terms: due on receipt.

3 Add a new vendor – Staples, 101 Main St., San Diego, CA 92600 terms: due on receipt.

4 Add a new account – category type: Credit Card, detail type: Credit Card, name: AMEX.

5 Add a new account – category type: Other Current Assets, detail type: Other Current Assets, name: Supplies Asset.

6 Add a new tracked product – name/description: Sport Cub S, initial quantity on hand: 0, inventory asset account: Inventory Asset, price: 600.00, cost: 479.00, income account: Sales, expense account: Cost of Goods Sold.

7 Add a new tracked product – name/description: Mystique RES, initial quantity on hand: 0, inventory asset account: Inventory Asset, price: 450.00, cost: 325.00, income account: Sales, expense account: Cost of Goods Sold.

8 Record a new purchase order for products on 1/2/19 – vendor: E-flite, product 1: Sport Cub S, QTY: 5, product 2: Mystique RES, QTY: 3.

9 Record a new purchase order for products on 1/3/19 – vendor: Kyosho, product 1: Broon F830 Ride, QTY: 4, product 2: GO Aircraft Radio, QTY: 2, product 3: Seawind Carbon Sailboat, QTY: 1.

10 Record a new bill based on a purchase order #1001 on 1/7/19 – vendor: E-flite, terms: Net 15. All items ordered were received.

11 Record a new bill without a purchase order on 1/8/19 – new vendor: San Diego News-Press, terms: Net 15, account: Advertising, amount: 500.00.

12 Record a new bill without a purchase order on 1/10/19 – new vendor: Gomez Insurance, terms: Net 15, account 1: Insurance, amount: 400.00, account 2: Prepaid Expenses, amount: 4,400.00.

13 Pay bill due to Kyosho on 1/18/19 using the checking account and starting with check no. 1001.

14 Record a credit card charge on 1/11/19, vendor: Village Steak House, using credit card: AMEX, account: Meals and Entertainment, amount: 240.00.

15 Record check on 1/14/19, no.: 1002, vendor: Staples, amount: 450.00, account: Supplies Asset.

16 Open your previously customized report named Trial Balance 1/31/19. Your report should look like Figure 5.21.

Figure 5.21

Trial Balance (as of 1/31/19)

Case 2
TRIAL BALANCE
As of January 31, 2019

	DEBIT	CREDIT
Checking	7,150.00	
Accounts Receivable	1,425.00	
Inventory Asset	5,410.00	
Prepaid Expenses	6,800.00	
Supplies Asset	450.00	
Undeposited Funds	925.00	
Machinery & Equipment:Depreciation		1,000.00
Machinery & Equipment:Original cost	10,000.00	
Accounts Payable		8,670.00
AMEX		240.00
Notes Payable		12,000.00
Common Stock		100.00
Opening Balance Equity		0.00
Retained Earnings		8,385.00
Sales		5,700.00
Services		225.00
Cost of Goods Sold	3,020.00	
Advertising	500.00	
Insurance	400.00	
Meals and Entertainment	240.00	
TOTAL	$36,320.00	$36,320.00

17 Create and print a Transaction Report for the Checking account as you did earlier in the chapter.

18 Create and print a Transaction Report for the Inventory Asset account as you did earlier in the chapter.

19 Create and print a Transaction Report for the Accounts Payable (A/P) account as you did earlier in the chapter.

20 If your trial balance differs from what is in Figure 5.21, do the following:

   a.   Make sure that all of your changes were dated in January 2019.

   b.   View the Transaction Reports you created to locate any errors.

   c.   Ask your instructor for assistance.

   d.   Be sure your company matches the above since, in the following chapter, you will add additional business events.

21 Export your Trial Balance report to Excel and save it with the file name: Student Name (replace with your name) Ch 05 Case 02 Trial Balance.xlsx.

22 Open and print the custom report you created in the last chapter called Transaction Detail by Account.

23 Export your Transactions Detail by Account report to Excel and save it with the file name: Student Name (replace with your name) Ch 05 Case 02 Transaction Detail by Account.xlsx.

24 Sign out of your company.

Case 3

Now it's time for you to add some operating activities (purchases, credit card charges, and cash payments) to your company.

Based on what you learned in the text, using the Sample Company, you are to add the following transactions to your company:

1 Add a new vendor – Google, Inc., 1600 Amphitheatre Parkway, Mountain View, CA 94043, terms: Net 15.

2 Add a new vendor – Samsung, Inc., 105 Challenger Rd., Ridgefield Park, NJ 07660, terms: Net 15.

3 Add a new vendor – Staples, Inc., 101 Main St., San Diego, CA 92600, terms: Net 30.

4 Modify Apple, Inc. (existing Vendor) – Name should be Apple Computer, Inc., address: 1 Infinite Loop Cupertino, CA 95014, terms: Net 15.

5 Add a new account – category type: Credit Card, detail type: Credit Card, name: AMEX.

6 Add a new account – category type: Other Current Assets, detail type: Other Current Assets, name: Supplies Asset.

7 Add a new taxable product – Name/Sales & Purchase information: Samsung Galaxy 8, initial quantity on hand: 0, inventory asset account: Inventory Asset, Sales price: 450.00, cost: 350.00, income account: Sales of Product Income, expense account: Cost of Goods Sold. (Use your current system date as the "as of date".)

8 Add a new taxable product – Name/Sales & Purchase information: Samsung Note, initial quantity on hand: 0, inventory asset account: Inventory Asset, Sales price: 850.00, cost: 650.00, income account: Sales of Product Income, expense account: Cost of Goods Sold. (Use your current system date as the "as of date".)

9 Record a new purchase order (1001) for products on 1/6/20 – vendor: Google, Inc., Pixel QTY: 10

10 Record a new purchase order (1002) for products on 1/7/20 – vendor: Samsung, Inc., product 1: Samsung Galaxy 8, QTY: 5, product 2: Samsung Note, QTY: 8.

11 Record a new bill based on a purchase order #1001 dated 1/6/20 – vendor: Google, Inc., terms: Net 15. All items ordered were received on 1/10/20 (the bill date).

12 Record a new bill without a purchase order on 1/8/20 – new vendor: News-Press, terms: Net 15, account: Advertising, amount: 1,300.00.

13 Record a new bill without a purchase order on 1/10/20 – new vendor: Hathaway Insurance, terms: Net 15, account 1: Insurance, amount: 300.00, account 2: Prepaid Expenses, amount: 3,300.00.

14 Pay bill due to Apple Computer, Inc. on 1/18/20 using the checking account and starting with check no. 321.

15 Record a credit card charge on 1/11/20, new vendor: Village Steak House, using credit card: AMEX, account: Meals and Entertainment, amount: 123.00.

16 Record check on 1/14/20, no.: 322, vendor: Staples, amount: 327.00, account: Supplies Asset.

17 Open and print your previously customized report named Trial Balance 1/31/20. Your report should look like Figure 5.22.

Figure 5.22

Trial Balance as of 1/31/20

Case 3 - Student Name (ID number)

TRIAL BALANCE

As of January 31, 2020

	DEBIT	CREDIT
Checking	15,853.00	
Accounts Receivable (A/R)	2,610.00	
Inventory Asset	5,700.00	
Prepaid Expenses	6,060.00	
Supplies Asset	327.00	
Undeposited Funds	0.00	
Machinery & Equipment:Depreciation		2,000.00
Machinery & Equipment:Original cost	15,000.00	
Accounts Payable (A/P)		6,900.00
AMEX		123.00
State Board of Equalization Payable		675.00
Notes Payable		23,000.00
Opening Balance Equity		0.00
Owner's Equity		10,075.00
Sales of Product Income		6,750.00
Services		240.00
Cost of Goods Sold	4,500.00	
Advertising	1,300.00	
Insurance	300.00	
Meals and Entertainment	123.00	
TOTAL	**$51,763.00**	**$51,763.00**

18 Create and print a Transaction Report for the Checking account like you did in the chapter.

19 Create and print a Transaction Report for the Accounts Receivable (A/R) account.

20 Create and print a Transaction Report for the Inventory Asset account like you did in the chapter.

21 Create and print a Transaction Report for the Accounts Payable (A/P) account like you did in the chapter.

22 If your trial balance is different than Figure 5.21:

a. Make sure that all of your changes were dated in January 2020.

b. View the Transaction Reports you just created to locate any errors.

c. Ask your instructor for assistance.

d. Be sure your company matches the above, as in the following chapter you'll be adding additional business events.

23 Export your Trial Balance report to Excel and save it with the file name: Student Name (replace with your name) Ch 05 Case 03 Trial Balance.xlsx.

24 Open and print the custom report you created in the last chapter called Transaction Detail by Account.

25 Export your Transactions Detail by Account report to Excel and save it with the file name: Student Name (replace with your name) Ch 05 Case 03 Transaction Detail by Account.xlsx.

26 Sign out of your company.

6

Investing and Financing Activities

Upon completion of this chapter, the student will be able to do the following:

- Record the acquisition of a fixed asset
- Record the acquisition of a long-term investment
- Record the sale of common stock
- Record the payment of a dividend
- Record a long-term borrowing (long-term debt)
- Record payment on long-term borrowing (long-term debt)
- Record the acquisition of a fixed asset by taking on new debt

Overview

Intuit has provided a sample company online to provide new users a test drive of its QBO product. In this chapter, you will open this sample company and practice various features of QBO. You will be recording investing activities such as acquiring a long-term investment and a fixed asset to the Sample Company file. In addition, you will be recording financing activities, such as selling common stock, paying a dividend, borrowing on a long-term basis, and making payments on long-term debt to the Sample Company file. Lastly, you will record an investing activity, acquiring a new fixed asset, and a financing activity by borrowing funds to purchase the fixed asset. Remember, if you stop in the middle of this work, none of your work will be saved. So when you return, the same sample company, without your work, will appear. In some parts of the chapter, you'll be asked to sign out of the Sample Company and sign back in so the Sample Company is reset to its original state. In the end of chapter work, you will be asked to perform the same tasks completed on the Sample Company on your Student Company. That work, of course, will be saved.

Fixed Assets

In this section, you will be recording the acquisition of fixed assets. Fixed assets are long-term tangible property that a firm owns and uses in the production of its income and is not expected to be consumed or converted into cash any sooner than at least one year's time. Normally, a fixed asset's cost is depreciated over time as a means of allocating its cost over its useful life. The depreciation is recorded to a depreciation expense account and added to an accumulated depreciation (contra-asset) account. That process will be explained in the chapter on adjusting entries.

To add an asset, you will use the Check task accessed by clicking the Create (+) icon. Alternatively, you could purchase new fixed assets with using a credit card or take on new debt. The Sample Company had a fixed asset account for trucks, which you'll use to record the purchase of a truck. If you were to purchase some other type of fixed asset, equipment for example, you would need to create a new fixed asset account named Equipment and two additional subaccounts to the Equipment account: Original Cost and Accumulated Depreciation.

To record the purchase of a new truck and new equipment in the Sample Company, do the following:

1 Open your Internet browser.

2 Type **https://qbo.intuit.com/redir/testdrive** into your browser's address text box and then press [**Enter**] to view the Sample Company Home page.

3 Click the **Create (+)** icon and then click **Check**.

4 Select + **add new** from the drop-down list in the Choose a payee text box.

5 Type **Sunset Auto** in the Name text box, select **Vendor** as the Type, and click **Save**.

6 Accept the given Payment date and Check no. provided by QBO.

7 Type **Truck:Original Cost** in the Account column of line 1.

8 Type **2,500.00** in the Amount column of line 1 and the press [**Tab**]. Your screen should look like Figure 6.1.

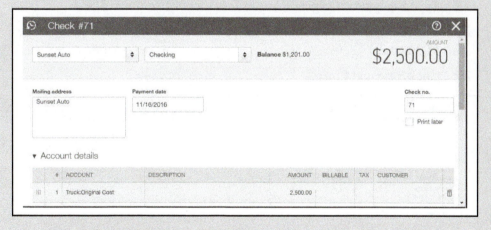

Figure 6.1

Purchase of Truck

9 Click **Save and New**.

10 Select **Tania's Nursery** from the drop-down list in the Choose a payee text box.

11 Select + **Add new** from the drop-down list in Account column of line 1.

12 Select **Fixed Assets** from the drop-down list in the Category type text box.

13 Select **Machinery & Equipment** from the drop-down list in the Detail type text box.

14 Type **Equipment** in the Name text box, and click **Save and New**.

15 Select **Fixed Assets** from the drop-down list in the Category type text box.

16 Select **Machinery & Equipment** from the drop-down list in the Detail type text box.

17 Type **Original Cost** in the Name text box.

18 Place a check in the **Is sub-account** check box.

19 Select **Equipment** from the drop-down list of accounts under the Is sub-account check box.

20 Click **Save and New**.

21 Select **Fixed Assets** from the drop-down list in the Category type text box.

22 Select **Accumulated Depreciation** from the drop-down list in the Detail type text box.

23 Type **Accumulated Depreciation** in the Name text box.

24 Place a check in the **Is sub-account** check box.

25 Select **Equipment** from the drop-down list of accounts under the Is sub-account check box.

26 Click **Save and Close**.

27 Type **Equipment:Original Cost** in the Account column of line 1.

28 Type **1,000** in the Amount column of line 1 and then press [**Tab**] to see Figure 6.2.

29 Click **Save and Close**.

Figure 6.2

Purchase of Equipment

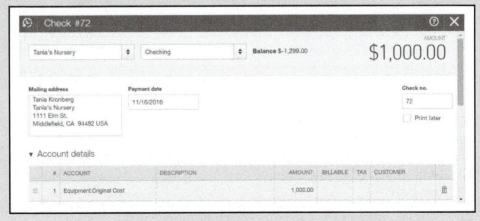

You have recorded the purchase of two new fixed assets.

Long-Term Investments

The acquisition of a long-term investment is another type of investing activity. In general, a long-term investment is the purchase of a financial instrument (bond, common stock, and preferred stock) that matures in more than one year.

To record the purchase of a long-term investment in the Sample Company, do the following:

1 Continue from where you left off. If you closed the Sample Company, follow the steps to reopen it found at the beginning of this chapter.

2 Click the **Create** (+) icon, and select **Check**.

3 Select + **add new** from the drop-down list in the Choose a payee text box.

4 Type **Scottrade** in the Name text box, select **Vendor** as the Type, and click **Save.**

5 Accept the given Payment date and Check no. provided by QBO.

6 Select + **add new** from the drop-down list in Account column of line 1.

7 Select **Other Assets** from the drop-down list in the Category Type text box.

8 Select **Other Long-term Assets** from the drop-down list in the Detail type text box.

9 Type **Investments** in the Name text box, and click **Save and Close**.

10 Type **3,000** in the Amount column of line 1 and then press [**Tab**] to see Figure 6.3.

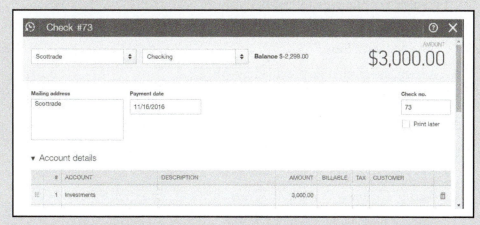

Figure 6.3

Purchase of a Long-Term Investment

11 Click **Save and Close**.

12 Click the **Gear** icon, and click **Sign out** to reset the Sample Company.

You have recorded the purchase of a long-term investment.

Common Stock and Dividends

The sale of common stock and the payment of cash dividends to shareholders are two common financing activities. Common stock is a stockholders' equity account. Dividends are a distribution of earnings to shareholders and are accounted for as a reduction in retained earnings. Both of these are cash activities in that the sale of stock results in a cash receipt (you will account for it as a bank deposit), whereas the payment of a cash dividend results in a cash payment. Two previous payments from customers appear when you attempt to record a bank deposit from the issuance of stock. These payments have been received but not recorded. Ignore those for now. To simplify this transaction, we will assume that the common stock is no-par common stock, and thus, no additional paid-in capital exists. Also, we'll assume that the declaration, record, and payment dates are all the same.

To record the sale of stock and payment of cash dividends in the Sample Company, do the following:

1   Open your Internet browser.

2   Type **https://qbo.intuit.com/redir/testdrive** into your browser's address text box, and press [**Enter**] to view the Sample Company Home page. (Do not continue from the previous work as the Sample Company file needs to be reset to its original state.)

3   Click the **Create** (+) icon and then select **Bank Deposit**.

4   Select + **Add new** from the drop-down list in the Received From column of line 1 in the Add New Deposits section. The Add New Deposits section is below the Select Existing Payments section so you may have to scroll down the page to find it.

5   Type **WB Investments** in the Name text box, select **Vendor** in the Type box, and click **Save**.

6   Accept the given date provided by QBO.

7   Select + **Add new** from the drop-down list in the Account column of line 1.

8   Select **Equity** from the drop-down list in the **Category type** text box.

9   Select **Common Stock** from the drop-down list in the **Detail type** text box.

10   Accept **Common Stock** in the **Name** text box, and click **Save and Close**.

11   Select **Check** as the Payment Method.

12   Type **10,000** in the Amount column of line 1, and press [**Tab**]. Your screen should look like Figure 6.4.

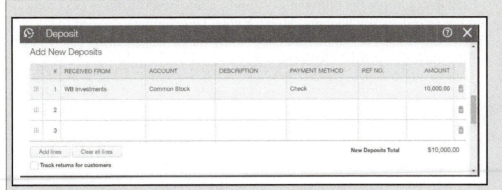

Figure 6.4

Recording the Deposit of Funds from the Sale of Common Stock

13 Click **Save and Close**.

14 Click the **Create** (+) icon, and select **Check**.

15 Select + **Add new** from the drop-down list in the **Choose a payee** text box.

16 Type **Shareholders** in the Name text box, select **Vendor** in the Type box, and click **Save**.

17 Accept the given Payment date and Check no. provided by QBO.

18 Select **Retained Earnings** from the drop-down list in the Account column of line 1.

19 Type **1,250** in the Amount column of line 1, and press [**Tab**]. Your screen should look like Figure 6.5.

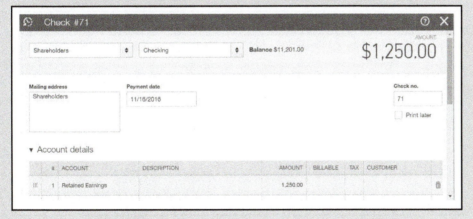

Figure 6.5

Payment of Dividends

20 Click **Save and Close**.

21 Do not sign out of the Sample Company.

Long-Term Debt

The borrowing of funds on a long-term basis and the repayment of debt are two additional financing activities. Both of these are cash activities in that the borrowing of funds results in a cash receipt (you will account for it as a bank deposit), whereas the payment of the debt results in a cash payment. There are two previous payments from customers that appear when you attempt to record a bank deposit from the borrowing of funds. These payments have been received but not recorded. You'll ignore those for now. This company decided to take the funds from the stock sale recorded above and the new borrowings below to pay off the old long-term debt with interest.

To record the receipt of funds from borrowing and the payment of long-term debt in the Sample Company, do the following:

1   Continue from where you left off. If you closed the Sample Company, follow the steps to reopen it found at the beginning of this chapter.

2   Click the **Create (+)** icon and then select **Bank Deposit**.

3   Select **+ Add new** from the drop-down list in the Received From column of line 1 in the Add New Deposits section.

4   Type **Bank of La Jolla** in the Name text box, select **Vendor** in the Type box, and click **Save**.

5   Accept the given date provided by QBO.

6   Select **Notes Payable** from the drop-down list in Account column of line 1.

7   Select **Check** from the drop-down list in the Payment Method column of line 1.

8   Type **15,000** in the Amount column of line 1, and press **[Tab]**. Your screen should look like Figure 6.6.

Figure 6.6

Recording the Deposit of Funds from Borrowing

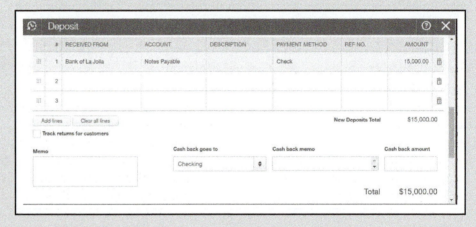

9   Click **Save and Close**.

10   Click the **Create (+)** icon, and select **Check**.

11   Select **+ Add new** from the drop-down list in the Choose a payee text box.

12   Type **Bank of San Diego** in the Name text box, select **Vendor** in the Type box, and click **Save**.

13   Accept the given Payment date and Check no. provided by QBO.

14   Select **Notes Payable** from the drop-down list in the Account column of line 1.

15 Type **25,000** in the Amount column of line 1 and then press [**Tab**].

16 Select **+ Add new** from the drop-down list in the Account column of line 2.

17 Select **Expenses** from the drop-down list in the Category Type text box.

18 Select **Interest Paid** from the drop-down list in the Detail Type text box.

19 Type **Interest Expense** in the Name text box and click **Save and Close**.

20 Type **1,000** in the Amount column of line 2, and press [**Tab**]. Your screen should look like Figure 6.7.

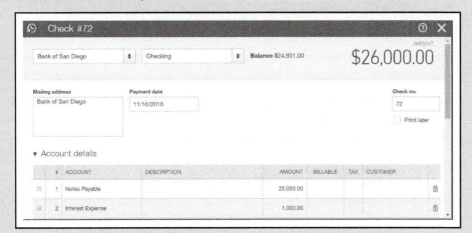

Figure 6.7

Repayment of Long-Term Debt with Interest

21 Click **Save and Close.**

22 Do not sign out of the Sample Company.

Acquisition of a Fixed Asset in Exchange for Long-Term Debt

You completed the process for recording an investing activity (purchase of a fixed asset) and a financing activity (borrowing on a long-term basis). Both of these transactions were recorded by affecting the checking account (cash).

Occasionally, a company acquires a fixed asset by issuing long-term debt, for example, purchasing another truck in exchange for a note payable. This cannot be recorded using the checking account since no funds were exchanged. Instead, you will use the journal entry process to record the fixed asset acquisition and the long-term debt borrowing.

To record the purchase of a fixed asset by issuing debt, do the following:

1 Continue from where you left off. If you closed the Sample Company, follow the steps to reopen it found at the beginning of this chapter.

2 Click the **Create (+)** icon, and select **Journal Entry.**

3 Accept the Journal date and Journal no. provided by QBO.

4 Select **Truck: Original Cost** from the drop-down list in the Account column of line 1.

5 Type **3,400** in the Debits column of line 1.

6 Select **Notes Payable** from the drop-down list in the Account column of line 2.

7 Accept **3,400** in the Credits column of line 2, and press [**Tab**] to view the journal entry shown in Figure 6.8.

Figure 6.8

Journal Entry to Record Purchase of Fixed Asset in Exchange for Long-Term Debt

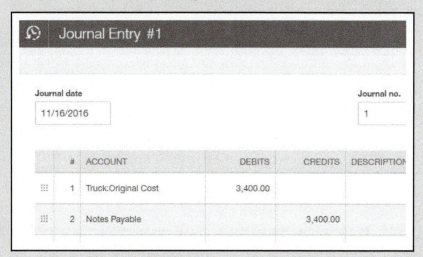

8 Click **Save and Close**.

9 Sign out of the Sample Company.

End Note

In this chapter, you recorded investing activities: the acquisition of fixed assets and of long-term investments, the sale of common stocks, the payment of a dividend, the borrowing and payment of long-term debt, and the acquisition of fixed assets by taking on new debt. In the next chapter, you will work with payroll.

Chapter 6 Questions

1   What are the steps to record the acquisition of a fixed asset using a check?

2   What are the steps to record the acquisition of a fixed asset for a note payable?

3   What are the steps to record the sale of common stock?

4   What are the steps to record the payment of dividends?

5   What are the steps to record borrowing on a note payable?

Chapter 6 Matching

a. Operating activity

b. Investing activity

c. Financing activity

d. Fixed assets

e. Long-term investment

f. Common stock

g. Dividends

h. Long-term debt

i. Bank deposit

j. Journal entry

_____ Long-term tangible property that a firm owns

_____ Distribution of earnings to shareholders

_____ A stockholders' equity account

_____ Used to record purchase of a fixed asset for a note

_____ A 5-year note payable

_____ Sales receipt

_____ A financial instrument that matures in more than 1 year

_____ Used to record amounts received from a note payable

_____ Sale of common stock

_____ Purchase of common stock

Chapter 6 Cases

The following cases require you to open the company you updated in Chapter 5. Each of the following cases is continued throughout the text in a sequential manner. For example, if you are assigned Case 01, you will use the file you modified in this chapter in all following chapters. Each of the following cases is similar in concepts assessed but differs in amounts and transactions.

To reopen your company, do the following:

1   Open your Internet browser.

2   Type **https://qbo.intuit.com/qbo28/loginwebredir** into your browser's address text box.

3   Type your User ID and Password into the text boxes as you have done before.

Case 1

Now add some investing and financing activities to your company.

Based on what you learned in the text and using the Sample Company, you are to add the following transactions to your company:

1   Create three new fixed asset accounts: category type: Fixed Asset, detail type: Machinery & Equipment and Accumulated Depreciation (where appropriate), account names: Equipment, Original Cost (a sub-account of Equipment), and Accumulated Depreciation (a sub-account of Equipment).

2   Create a new asset account with a category type: Other Assets, detail type: Other Long-Term Assets, name: Investments.

3   Record the purchase of a new computer on 1/10/18 from Office Depot, check: 1003, amount: $1,375.00, account: Equipment:Original Cost.

4   Record a long-term investment on 1/11/18 to Etrade (a new vendor), check 1004, amount: $4,000, account: Investments.

5   Record the sale of common stock on 1/12/18 to Shareholders (a new vendor), deposit amount: $20,000, account: Common Stock.

6   Record the payment of dividends to Shareholders on 1/15/18, check 1005, in the amount of $500.

7   Record the deposit of funds from a new note payable signed on 1/16/18 with Bank of CA (a new vendor) in the amount of $65,000.

8   Record the payment to Rabo Bank (a new vendor) to retire an existing note payable on 1/16/18 of $60,000 with interest of $600 using check 1006.

9   Record the purchase of an additional computer on 1/17/18 from Office Depot in exchange for a note payable of $1,800.

10   Open your previously customized report named Trial Balance 1/31/18. Your report should look like Figure 6.9.

11   Create and print a Transaction Report for the Checking account.

12   Create and print a Transaction Report for the Equipment:Original Cost account.

13   Create and print a Transaction Report for the Notes Payable account.

14   Create and print a Transaction Report for the Common Stock account.

15   If your trial balance differs from Figure 6.9, do the following:

a.   Make sure that all of your changes were dated in January 2018.

b.   View the Transaction Reports you just created to locate any errors.

c.   Ask your instructor for assistance.

d.   Be sure your company matches the above, as in the following chapter you'll be adding additional business events.

Figure 6.9

Trial Balance as of 1/31/18

Case 1
TRIAL BALANCE
As of January 31, 2018

	DEBIT	CREDIT
Checking	34,850.00	
Accounts Receivable	1,030.00	
Inventory Asset	11,800.00	
Prepaid Expenses	8,000.00	
Supplies Asset	375.00	
Undeposited Funds	5,000.00	
Equipment:Original Cost	3,175.00	
Furniture & Fixtures:Depreciation		10,000.00
Furniture & Fixtures:Original cost	40,000.00	
Investments	4,000.00	
Accounts Payable		7,645.00
VISA		1,800.00
Notes Payable		66,800.00
Common Stock		21,000.00
Opening Balance Equity		0.00
Retained Earnings		5,000.00
Sales		2,160.00
Services		170.00
Cost of Goods Sold	1,300.00	
Interest Expense	600.00	
Rent or Lease	2,500.00	
Travel	1,800.00	
Utilities	145.00	
TOTAL	$114,575.00	$114,575.00

16 Export your Trial Balance report to Excel, and save it with the file name: Student Name (replace with your name) Ch 06 Case 01 Trial Balance.xlsx.

17 Open and print the custom report you created in the last chapter called Transaction Detail by Account.

18 Export your Transactions Detail by Account report to Excel, and save it with the file name: Student Name (replace with your name) Ch 06 Case 01 Transaction Detail by Account.xlsx.

19 Sign out of your company.

Case 2

Now add some investing and financing activities to your company.

Based on what you learned in the text and using the Sample Company, you are to add the following transactions to your company:

1 Create three new fixed asset accounts: category type: Fixed Asset, detail type: Furniture & Fixtures and Accumulated Depreciation (where appropriate), account names: Furniture, Original Cost (a sub-account of Furniture), and Accumulated Depreciation (a sub-account of Furniture).

2   Create a new asset account with a category type: Other Assets, detail type: Other Long-Term Assets, name: Investments.

3   Record the purchase of new furniture on 1/11/19 from Staples, check: 1003, amount: $2,250.00, account: Furniture:Original Cost.

4   Record a long-term investment on 1/11/19 to Raymond James (a new vendor), check 1004, amount: $3,200, account: Investments.

5   Record the sale of common stock on 1/14/19 to Shareholders (a new vendor), deposit amount: $25,000, account: Common Stock.

6   Record the payment of dividends to Shareholders on 1/15/19, check 1005, in the amount of $800.

7   Record the deposit of funds from a new note payable signed on 1/16/19 with Bank of T J (a new vendor) in the amount of $25,000.

8   Record the payment to Community Bank (a new vendor) to retire an existing note payable on 1/16/19 of $12,000 with interest of $300 using check 1006.

9   Record the purchase of additional furniture from Staples on 1/17/19 in exchange for a note payable of $2,625.

10   Open your previously customized report named Trial Balance 1/31/19. Your report should look like Figure 6.10.

Figure 6.10

Trial Balance as of 1/31/19

Case 2
TRIAL BALANCE
As of January 31, 2019

	DEBIT	CREDIT
Checking	38,600.00	
Accounts Receivable	1,425.00	
Inventory Asset	5,410.00	
Prepaid Expenses	6,800.00	
Supplies Asset	450.00	
Undeposited Funds	925.00	
Furniture:Original Cost	4,875.00	
Machinery & Equipment:Depreciation		1,000.00
Machinery & Equipment:Original cost	10,000.00	
Investments	3,200.00	
Accounts Payable		8,670.00
AMEX		240.00
Notes Payable		27,625.00
Common Stock		25,100.00
Opening Balance Equity		0.00
Retained Earnings		7,585.00
Sales		5,700.00
Services		225.00
Cost of Goods Sold	3,020.00	
Advertising	500.00	
Insurance	400.00	
Interest Expense	300.00	
Meals and Entertainment	240.00	
TOTAL	**$76,145.00**	**$76,145.00**

11 Create and print a Transaction Report for the Checking account.

12 Create and print a Transaction Report for the Furniture:Original Cost account.

13 Create and print a Transaction Report for the Notes Payable account.

14 Create and print a Transaction Report for the Common Stock account.

15 If your trial balance differs from Figure 6.10, do the following:

    a. Make sure that all of your changes were dated in January 2019.

    b. View the Transaction Reports you created to locate any errors.

    c. Ask your instructor for assistance.

    d. Be sure your company matches the above, because in the following chapter, you will be adding additional business events.

16 Export your Trial Balance report to Excel, and save it with the file name: Student Name (replace with your name) Ch 06 Case 02 Trial Balance.xlsx.

17 Open and print the custom report you created in the last chapter called Transaction Detail by Account.

18 Export your Transactions Detail by Account report to Excel, and save it with the file name: Student Name (replace with your name) Ch 06 Case 02 Transaction Detail by Account.xlsx.

19 Sign out of your company.

Case 3

Now it's time for you to add some investing and financing activities to your company.

Based on what you learned in the text, using the Sample Company, you are to add the following transactions to your company:

1 Create three new fixed asset accounts. Each are category type: Fixed Asset, detail type: Buildings and Accumulated Depreciation (where appropriate), account names: Buildings, Original Cost (a sub-account of Buildings), and Accumulated Depreciation (a sub-account of Buildings).

2 Create a new asset account with a category type: Other Assets, detail type: Other Long-Term Assets, name: Investments.

3 Create a new equity account with a category type: Equity, detail type: Common Stock, and name: Common Stock.

4 Record the purchase of a new equipment on 1/12/20 from Staples, Inc., check: 323, amount: $3,000.00, account: Machinery & Equipment: Original Cost.

5 Record a long-term investment on 1/13/20 to Etrade (a new vendor), check 324, amount: $5,700.00, account: Investments.

6 Record the sale of common stock on 1/14/20 to Shareholders (a new vendor) after receiving a check that was immediately deposited in the amount: $40,000.00 to account: Common Stock.

7 Record the deposit of funds from a new note payable signed on 1/16/20 with Chase Bank (a new vendor) in the amount of $32,000.00.

8 Record the payment to Rabobank (a new vendor) to retire an existing note payable on 1/17/20 of $23,000 with interest of $300 using check 325 for a total of $23,300.

9 Record the purchase of a building from Leeds, Inc. (a new vendor) on 1/17/20 in exchange for a note payable of $31,800.00.

10 Open and print your previously customized report named Trial Balance 1/31/20. Your report should look like Figure 6.11.

Figure 6.11

Trial Balance as of 1/31/20

Case 3 - Student Name (ID number)

TRIAL BALANCE
As of January 31, 2020

	DEBIT	CREDIT
Checking	55,853.00	
Accounts Receivable (A/R)	2,610.00	
Inventory Asset	5,700.00	
Prepaid Expenses	6,050.00	
Supplies Asset	327.00	
Undeposited Funds	0.00	
Buildings:Original cost	31,800.00	
Machinery & Equipment:Depreciation		2,000.00
Machinery & Equipment:Original cost	18,000.00	
Investments	5,700.00	
Accounts Payable (A/P)		8,900.00
AMEX		123.00
State Board of Equalization Payable		675.00
Notes Payable		63,800.00
Common Stock		40,000.00
Opening Balance Equity		0.00
Owner's Equity		10,075.00
Sales of Product Income		6,750.00
Services		240.00
Cost of Goods Sold	4,500.00	
Advertising	1,300.00	
Insurance	300.00	
Interest Expense	300.00	
Meals and Entertainment	123.00	
TOTAL	$132,563.00	$132,563.00

11   Create and print a Transaction Report for the Checking account.

12   Create and print a Transaction Report for the Buildings:Original Cost account.

13   Create and print a Transaction Report for the Notes Payable account.

14   Create and print a Transaction Report for the Common Stock account.

15   If your trial balance is different than Figure 6.11:

   a.   Make sure that all of your changes were dated in January 2019.

   b.   View the Transaction Reports you just created to locate any errors.

   c.   Ask your instructor for assistance.

   d.   Be sure your company matches the above, as in the following chapter you'll be adding additional business events.

16   Export your Trial Balance report to Excel and save it with the file name: Student Name (replace with your name) Ch 06 Case 03 Trial Balance.xlsx.

17   Open and print the custom report you created in the last chapter called Transaction Detail by Account.

18   Export your Transactions Detail by Account report to Excel and save it with the file name: Student Name (replace with your name) Ch 06 Case 03 Transaction Detail by Account.xlsx.

19   Sign out of your company.

7

Payroll

Upon completion of this chapter, the student will be able to do the following:

- Add a new employee
- Add payroll-related general ledger accounts
- Pay employees and record payroll expenses and liabilities

Overview

Intuit has provided a Sample Company online to let new users test drive its QBO product. In this chapter, you will open this Sample Company and practice payroll activities in QBO. QBO Payroll is an add-on feature to QBO. You can use a trial version of QBO Payroll, but it only lasts for 30 days. Even though the payroll features available through QBO Payroll are extensive and helpful, they focus on real companies and real-time frames. Thus, this chapter will focus on the creation of new employees, general ledger accounts, and payment to employees without the use of QBO Payroll.

Remember, if you stop in the middle of this work, none of your work will be saved. So, when you return, the same sample company, without your work, will appear. In some parts of the chapter, you will be asked to sign out of the Sample Company and sign back in so the Sample Company is reset to its original state. In the end of chapter work, you will be asked to perform the same tasks completed on the Sample Company on your Student Company. That work, of course, will be saved.

 ## Employees

In this section, you will be adding a new employee to QBO.

To add a new employee to the Sample Company, do the following:

1   Open your Internet browser.

2   Type **https://qbo.intuit.com/redir/testdrive** into your browser's address text box, and press **[Enter]** to view the Sample Company Home page.

3   Click the **Employees** menu in the navigation bar.

4   Click the **Add an employee** button.

5 Click the **Not right now** button when asked to Turn payroll on.

6 Type **Mae West** as the employee's name and provide the following address information: **2393 Ridge Place #3, Rancho Mar, CA, 93154**. Type **322-31-8999** as the Employee ID No. Your screen should look like Figure 7.1.

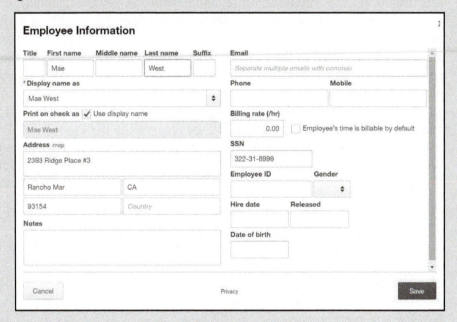

Figure 7.1

Employee Information (adding a new employee)

7 Click **Save**.

8 Your Employee window should now reflect three employees shown in Figure 7.2.

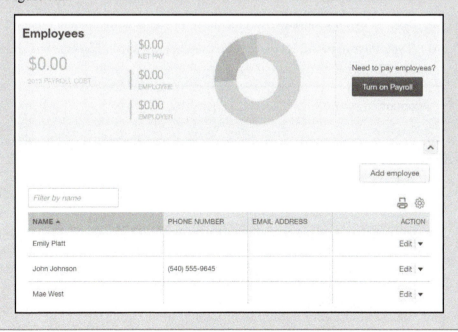

Figure 7.2

Employees

Payroll Accounts

Once again, if you were using QuickBooks Payroll Online, general ledger accounts to capture payroll information would be created for you in the setup process. However, since you are not using QuickBooks Payroll Online, you will have to create them on your own. To keep things simple, you can create the minimum two new accounts for payroll: Payroll (expense) and Payroll Tax Payable (liability).

An employer agrees to pay its employees a salary per month or an hourly rate. In either case, for the agreed upon salary or hourly rate times hours worked, amounts are recorded to the Payroll (expense) account. Depending on the state, employees are often required to have an estimated amount of federal and state income taxes withheld from their paychecks by their employers. In addition, employers must withhold social security (6.2%) and Medicare (1.45%) taxes. Amounts withheld from employees will be recorded in the Payroll Tax Payable (liability) account until remitted to the U.S. Treasury and state government entities. Employers must match those amounts for social security (6.2%) and Medicare (1.45%) taxes. These matching costs will be recorded as additional Payroll expense.

To add payroll-related accounts to the Sample Company, do the following:

1 Continue from where you left off. If you closed the Sample Company, follow the steps to reopen it found at the beginning of this chapter.

2 Click the **Gear** icon and then click **Chart of Accounts**.

3 Click **New**.

4 Select **Expenses** from the drop-down list in the **Category Type** text box.

5 Select **Payroll Expenses** from the drop-down list in the **Detail Type** text box.

6 Type **Payroll** in the Name text box replacing Payroll Expenses as shown in Figure 7.3.

Figure 7.3

Account (adding a new payroll account)

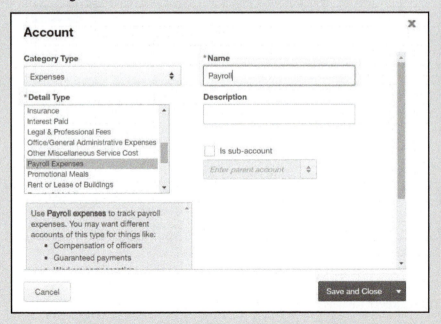

7   Click **Save and New**.

8   Select **Other Current Liabilities** from the drop-down list in the **Category Type** text box.

9   Select **Payroll Tax Payable** from the drop-down list in the **Detail Type** text box.

10   Accept **Payroll Tax Payable** in the **Name** text box.

11   Click **Save and Close**.

12   Do not sign out of the Sample Company.

You have added two payroll-related general ledger accounts.

Pay Employees

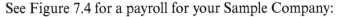

The payment of employees requires gathering information from each employee that helps determine withholding amounts and payroll expenses. The federal and state governments provide formulas and/or tables to help employers calculate these amounts. In this text, you will be provided these amounts. Additional taxes such as training, unemployment, etc., are ignored for this illustration. Since payroll is a recurring event, it will help to make these checks recur, which can be edited for each payroll for changes in hours worked where applicable. In this example payroll is paid semi-monthly.

See Figure 7.4 for a payroll for your Sample Company:

Pay/Tax/Withholding	Emily	John	Mae	Total
Hours if applicable	n/a	80	60	
Annual salary or hourly rate	$ 60,000	$ 18.00	$ 18.00	
Gross pay	**2,500.00**	**1,440.00**	**1,080.00**	**5,020.00**
Federal withholding	342.50	197.28	147.96	687.74
Social security employee (6.2%)	155.00	89.28	66.96	311.24
Medicare employee (1.45%)	36.25	20.88	15.66	72.79
Employee withholding	**533.75**	**307.44**	**230.58**	**1,071.77**
Social security employer (6.2%)	155.00	89.28	66.96	311.24
Medicare company employer (1.45%)	36.25	20.88	15.66	72.79
Employer payroll tax expense	**191.25**	**110.16**	**82.62**	**384.03**
Net Check amount	1,966.25	1,132.56	849.42	3,948.23

Figure 7.4

Semi-Monthly Payroll Information

To record the payment of employees in the Sample Company, do the following:

1   Continue from where you left off.

2   Click the **Create** (+) icon, and select **Check**.

3   Select **Emily Platt** from the drop-down list (Note: Employees are located at the bottom of the list.) in the **Choose a payee** text box.

4   Accept the given date and check number QBO provides.

5   Select **Payroll** from the drop-down list in Account column of line 1.

6   Type **2,500** in the Amount column of line 1 and press [**Tab**] four times.

7   Select **Payroll Tax Payable** from the drop-down list in Account column of line 2.

8   Type **−533.75** in the Amount column of line 1 and press [**Tab**] four times. (Be sure to enter this amount as a negative number.)

9   Select **Payroll** from the drop-down list in Account column of line 3.

10 Type **191.25** in the Amount column of line 3 and press [**Tab**] four times.

11 Select **Payroll Tax Payable** from the drop-down list in Account column of line 4.

12 Type **−191.25** in the Amount column of line 4 and press [**Tab**] four times. (Be sure to enter this amount as a negative number.) Your screen should look like Figure 7.5.

Figure 7.5

Check #71 (paycheck for Emily Platt)

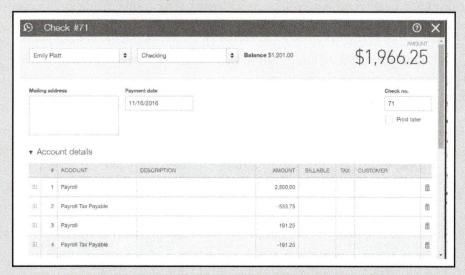

13 Click **Make Recurring** located at the bottom of the screen.

14 Select **Unscheduled** from the drop-down list in the **Type** text box.

15 Click **Save template**.

16 Click the **Gear** icon.

17 Select **Recurring Transactions** located in the List column.

18 Click **Use** located in the Action column. The check window will appear again completed like that shown in Figure 7.5.

19 Make sure the date is correct and then click **Save and New**.

20   Enter payroll information found in Figure 7.4 for John and Mae in the same way as you entered payroll information for Emily above. Be sure to make each of these unscheduled recurring events.

21   After entering the last check to record payroll above, click **Save and Close**.

22   Click **Reports** from the navigation bar.

23   Type **Trial Balance** in the Go to report search box and then press [**Enter**] to view a current trial balance, the top of which is shown in Figure 7.6.

Figure 7.6

Trial Balance (partial view)

Craig's Design and Landscaping Services

TRIAL BALANCE

As of November 16, 2016

	DEBIT	CREDIT
Checking		2,747.23
Savings	800.00	
Accounts Receivable (A/R)	5,281.52	
Inventory Asset	596.25	
Undeposited Funds	2,062.52	
Truck:Original Cost	13,495.00	
Accounts Payable (A/P)		1,602.67
Mastercard		157.72
Arizona Dept. of Revenue Payable		0.00
Board of Equalization Payable		370.94
Loan Payable		4,000.00
Payroll Tax Payable		1,455.80
Notes Payable		25,000.00
Opening Balance Equity	9,337.50	

24   Click the **2,747.23** amount on the Checking line to view a transaction report for the checking account shown in Figure 7.7. Note that this amount represents a credit balance in the account. Remember that this is a sample company created by Intuit and thus the balances may or many not make sense.

Figure 7.7

Transaction Report (checking account)

Craig's Design and Landscaping Services

TRANSACTION REPORT

November 1-16, 2016

DATE	TRANSACTION TYPE	NUM	NAME	MEMO/DESCRIPTION	ACCOUNT	SPLIT	AMOUNT	BALANCE
▾ Checking								
Beginning Balance								2,101.00
11/04/2016	Credit Card Credit				Checking	Mastercard	-900.00	1,201.00
11/16/2016	Check	73	Mae West		Checking	-Split-	-849.42	351.58
11/16/2016	Check	71	Emily Platt		Checking	-Split-	-1,966.25	-1,614.67
11/16/2016	Check	72	John Johnson		Checking	-Split-	-1,132.56	-2,747.23
Total for Checking							$ -4,848.23	
TOTAL							$ -4,848.23	

25 Match your screen with Figure 7.7, which may be in a different order than yours. (It shows different dates.)

26 Click **John Johnson** to view the payroll check shown in Figure 7.8.

Figure 7.8

Check #72 (John Johnson payroll check)

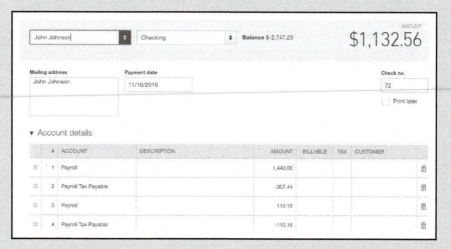

27 Match your screen to Figure 7.8, and close the check window.

28 Click **Back to report summary** to return to the Trial Balance report.

You have recorded payroll for one semi-monthly period. You can practice with another payroll using the recurring transactions you have set up.

29 Click the **Gear** icon, and click **Recurring transactions** located in the Lists column to view a list of recurring transactions shown in Figure 7.9. (If your list does not contain the three employees you recorded, you will need to return to these transactions, and click the Make recurring button.)

Figure 7.9

Recurring Transactions

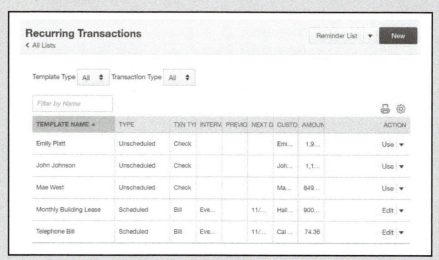

30 Click **Use** on the Mae West template to view a new payroll check for Mae.

31 Add 14 days to the **Payment date** text box representing the next semi-monthly period. In this example, the new date is 11/30/16; of course, yours will differ.

32 Payroll information for this next semi-monthly period is shown in Figure 7.10. Note the hours worked are different and John received an increase in his hourly rate.

Pay/Tax/Withholding	Emily	John	Mae	Total
Hours if applicable	n/a	75	63	
Annual salary or hourly rate	$ 60,000	$ 20.00	$ 18.00	
Gross pay	2,500.00	1,500.00	1,134.00	5,134.00
Federal withholding	342.50	205.50	155.36	703.36
Social security employee (6.2%)	155.00	93.00	70.31	318.31
Medicare employee (1.45%)	36.25	21.75	16.44	74.44
Employee withholding	533.75	320.25	242.11	1,096.11
Social security employer (6.2%)	155.00	93.00	70.31	318.31
Medicare company employer (1.45%)	36.25	21.75	16.44	74.44
Employer payroll tax expense	191.25	114.75	86.75	392.75
Net Check amount	1,966.25	1,179.75	891.89	4,037.89

Figure 7.10

Semi-Monthly Payroll Information

33 Type **1,134** in the Amount column on line 1.

34 Type **−242.11** in the Amount column on line 2.

35 Type **86.75** in the Amount column on line 3.

36 Type **−86.75** in the Amount column on line 4. Your screen should now look like Figure 7.11.

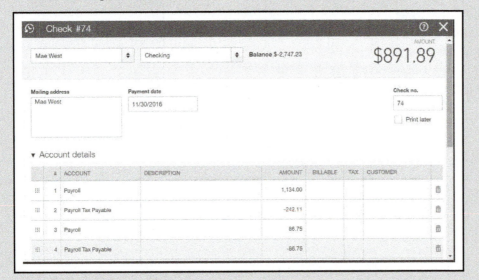

Figure 7.11

Check #74 (Mae West payroll check)

37 Click **Save and close**.

38 Use the same process (clicking **Use** from the Recurring Transactions list) for John and Emily to record their paychecks based on the new information shown in Figure 7.10. (Since Emily is salaried, her information remains the same each pay period, so nothing needs to be changed from the recurring transaction information provided.) Click **Yes** to accept a duplicate check number if QBO identifies that the check number you are proposing has been used.

39 Click **Reports** from the navigation bar.

40 Type **Trial Balance** in the Go to report search box, and press [**Enter**].

41 Change the To: date in the report to include whatever date you used to enter the most recent semi-monthly payroll. In our example, that date was 11/30/16. Your date will differ. When changed, click Run report to see a partial view of the trial balance shown in Figure 7.12.

Figure 7.12

Trial Balance (partial view)

Craig's Design and Landscaping Services

TRIAL BALANCE

As of November 30, 2016

	DEBIT	CREDIT
Checking		6,785.12
Savings	800.00	
Accounts Receivable (A/R)	5,281.52	
Inventory Asset	596.25	
Undeposited Funds	2,062.52	
Truck:Original Cost	13,495.00	
Accounts Payable (A/P)		1,602.67
Mastercard		157.72
Arizona Dept. of Revenue Payable		0.00
Board of Equalization Payable		370.94
Loan Payable		4,000.00
Payroll Tax Payable		2,944.66
Notes Payable		25,000.00
Opening Balance Equity	9,337.50	

42 Click the **6,785.12** amount on the Checking line to view a transaction report for the checking account shown in Figure 7.13.

Figure 7.13

Transaction Report (checking account)

Craig's Design and Landscaping Services

TRANSACTION REPORT

November 2016

DATE	TRANSACTION TYPE	NUM	NAME	MEMO/DESCRIPTION	ACCOUNT	SPLIT	AMOUNT	BALANCE
▼ Checking								
Beginning Balance								2,101.00
11/04/2016	Credit Card Credit				Checking	Mastercard	-900.00	1,201.00
11/16/2016	Check	72	John Johnson		Checking	-Split-	-1,132.56	68.44
11/16/2016	Check	71	Emily Platt		Checking	-Split-	-1,966.25	-1,897.81
11/16/2016	Check	73	Mae West		Checking	-Split-	-849.42	-2,747.23
11/30/2016	Check	74	Mae West		Checking	-Split-	-891.89	-3,639.12
11/30/2016	Check	75	John Johnson		Checking	-Split-	-1,179.75	-4,818.87
11/30/2016	Check	76	Emily Platt		Checking	-Split-	-1,966.25	-6,785.12
Total for Checking							$ -8,886.12	
TOTAL							$ -8,886.12	

43 Match your screen with Figure 7.13, which may be in a different order than yours. It will show different dates. Take note of any differences.

44 Click any payroll-related transaction if you want to drill down to the payroll check you recorded to see if you can fix any differences noted.

45 Fix any errors you discover.

46 Sign out of this Sample Company.

You have recorded two semi-monthly payroll checks for the Sample Company. Keep in mind that since you are not using QuickBooks Payroll Online, there are no employee records of earnings or taxes.

End Note

In this chapter, you added a new employee, a new payroll (expense) account, and a new payroll tax payable (liability) account and paid employees. In the next chapter, you will work with budgets and bank reconciliations.

Chapter 7 Questions

1   What are the steps to create a new employee?

2   What are the steps to create a new account?

3   What are the two minimum accounts needed to account for payroll?

4   What types of costs are included in the Payroll (expense) account?

5   What types of costs are included in the Payroll Tax Payable (liability) account?

Chapter 7 Matching

a. 6.2%

b. 1.45%

c. Payroll

d. Payroll tax payable

e. QBO Payroll

f. Gross pay

g. Recurring transactions

h. Transaction report

i. Unscheduled

j. Record as negative amounts

_____ Account used to record the liability for Federal income tax withheld

_____ An add-on feature to QBO

_____ Rate used to calculate an employee's Medicare tax

_____ Hours worked times hourly rate

_____ Use to more efficiently record periodic payroll

_____ Payroll tax payable

_____ Accessed by clicking an amount on the trial balance

_____ One type of recurring event

_____ Account used to record all payroll expenses

_____ Rate used to calculate an employee's social security tax

Chapter 7 Cases

The following cases require you to open the company you updated in Chapter 6. Each of the following cases continues throughout the text in a sequential manner. For example, if you are assigned Case 01, you will use the file you modified in this chapter in all following chapters. Each of the following cases is similar in concepts assessed but differs in amounts and transactions.

To reopen your company, do the following:

1   Open your Internet browser.

2   Type **https://qbo.intuit.com/qbo28/loginwebredir** into your browser's address text box.

3   Type your User ID and Password into the text boxes as you have done before.

Case 1

Do not install QBO Payroll. Based on what you learned in the text and using the Sample Company, you are to add the following payroll-related activities to your company:

1   Add two new accounts like you did in the chapter: Payroll (expense) and Payroll Tax Payable (liability).

2   Add a new employee: Ben Franklin, 32 Ocean View Lane, La Jolla, CA, 92037, social security number: 556-12-3467.

3   Add a second employee: Betsy Ross, 2323 1st Street, La Jolla, CA, 92037, social security number: 458-87-1974.

4   Payroll is paid twice a month on the 17th and the last day of each month.

5   Record payroll (as you did in the chapter) for 1/17/18 based on the information shown in Figure 7.14. After recording each employee's check, be sure to designate it as a recurring transaction.

Pay/Tax/Withholding	Ben	Betsy	Total
Hours if applicable	n/a	73	
Annual salary or hourly rate	$ 95,000	$ 21.50	
Gross pay	**3,958.33**	**1,569.50**	**5,527.83**
Federal withholding	542.29	215.02	**757.31**
Social security employee (6.2%)	245.42	97.31	**342.73**
Medicare employee (1.45%)	57.40	22.76	**80.16**
Employee withholding	**845.11**	**335.09**	**1,180.20**
Social security employer (6.2%)	245.42	97.31	**342.73**
Medicare company employer (1.45%)	57.40	22.76	**80.16**
Employer payroll tax expense	**302.82**	**120.07**	**422.89**
Net Check amount	3,113.22	1,234.41	**4,347.63**

Figure 7.14

Payroll Information (for 1/17/18)

6   Use the recurring transactions template you created above to help you record payroll (as you did in the chapter) for 1/31/18 based on the information shown in Figure 7.15.

Figure 7.15

Payroll Information (for 1/31/18)

Pay/Tax/Withholding	Ben	Betsy	Total
Hours if applicable	n/a	68	
Annual salary or hourly rate	$ 95,000	$ 21.50	
Gross pay	**3,958.33**	**1,462.00**	**5,420.33**
Federal withholding	542.29	200.29	**742.58**
Social security employee (6.2%)	245.42	90.64	**336.06**
Medicare employee (1.45%)	57.40	21.20	**78.60**
Employee withholding	**845.11**	**312.13**	**1,157.24**
Social security employer (6.2%)	245.42	90.64	**336.06**
Medicare company employer (1.45%)	57.40	21.20	**78.60**
Employer payroll tax expense	**302.82**	**111.84**	**414.66**
Net Check amount	3,113.22	1,149.87	**4,263.09**

7 Open your previously customized report named Trial Balance 1/31/18. Your report should look like Figure 7.16.

Figure 7.16

Trial Balance (as of 1/31/18)

	DEBIT	CREDIT
Checking	26,239.28	
Accounts Receivable	1,030.00	
Inventory Asset	11,800.00	
Prepaid Expenses	8,000.00	
Supplies Asset	375.00	
Undeposited Funds	5,000.00	
Equipment:Original Cost	3,175.00	
Furniture & Fixtures:Depreciation		10,000.00
Furniture & Fixtures:Original cost	40,000.00	
Investments	4,000.00	
Accounts Payable		7,645.00
Visa		1,800.00
Payroll Tax Payable		3,174.99
Notes Payable		66,800.00
Common Stock		21,000.00
Opening Balance Equity		0.00
Retained Earnings		5,000.00
Sales		2,160.00
Services		170.00
Cost of Goods Sold	1,300.00	
Interest Expense	600.00	
Payroll	11,785.71	
Rent or Lease	2,500.00	
Travel	1,800.00	
Utilities	145.00	
TOTAL	$117,749.99	$117,749.99

8   Create and print a Transaction Report for the Checking account.

9   Create and print a Transaction Report for the Payroll Tax Payable account.

10 If your trial balance differs from the one in Figure 7.16, do the following:

    a.   Make sure all of your changes were dated in January 2018.

    b.   View the Transaction Reports you created to locate any errors.

    c.   Ask your instructor for assistance.

    d.   Be sure your company matches the above since, in the following chapter, you will add additional business events.

11 Export your Trial Balance report to Excel, and save it with the file name: Student Name (replace with your name) Ch 07 Case 01 Trial Balance.xlsx.

12 Open and print the custom report you created in the last chapter called Transaction Detail by Account.

13 Export your Transactions Detail by Account report to Excel, and save it with the file name: Student Name (replace with your name) Ch 07 Case 01 Transaction Detail by Account.xlsx.

14 Sign out of your company.

Case 2

Do not install QBO Payroll. Based on what you learned in the text and using the Sample Company, you are to add the following payroll-related activities to your company:

1   Add two new accounts like you did in the chapter: Payroll (expense) and Payroll Tax Payable (liability).

2   Add a new employee: Frank Benjamin, 32 Ocean View Lane, La Jolla, CA, 92037, social security number: 556-12-3467.

3   Add a second employee: Sara Juarez, 2323 1st Street, La Jolla, CA, 92037, social security number: 458-87-1974.

4   Payroll is paid twice a month on the 16th and the last day of each month.

5   Record payroll (like you did in the chapter) for 1/16/19 based on the information shown in Figure 7.17. After recording each employee's check, be sure to designate it as a recurring transaction.

Figure 7.17

Payroll Information (for 1/16/19)

Pay/Tax/Withholding	Frank	Sara	Total
Hours if applicable	n/a	71	
Annual salary or hourly rate	$ 72,000	$ 18.75	
Gross pay	3,000.00	1,331.25	4,331.25
Federal withholding	411.00	182.38	593.38
Social security employee (6.2%)	186.00	82.54	268.54
Medicare employee (1.45%)	43.50	19.30	62.80
Employee withholding	640.50	284.22	924.72
Social security employer (6.2%)	186.00	82.54	268.54
Medicare company employer (1.45%)	43.50	19.30	62.80
Employer payroll tax expense	229.50	101.84	331.34
Net Check amount	2,359.50	1,047.03	3,406.53

6   Use the recurring transactions template you created above to help you record payroll (as you did in the chapter) for 1/31/19 based on the information shown in Figure 7.18.

Figure 7.18

Payroll Information (for 1/31/19)

Pay/Tax/Withholding	Frank	Sara	Total
Hours if applicable	n/a	66	
Annual salary or hourly rate	$ 72,000	$ 18.75	
Gross pay	3,000.00	1,237.50	4,237.50
Federal withholding	411.00	169.54	580.54
Social security employee (6.2%)	186.00	76.73	262.73
Medicare employee (1.45%)	43.50	17.94	61.44
Employee withholding	640.50	264.21	904.71
Social security employer (6.2%)	186.00	76.73	262.73
Medicare company employer (1.45%)	43.50	17.94	61.44
Employer payroll tax expense	229.50	94.67	324.17
Net Check amount	2,359.50	973.29	3,332.79

7 Open your previously customized report named Trial Balance 1/31/19. Your report should look like Figure 7.19.

Case 2
TRIAL BALANCE
As of January 31, 2019

	DEBIT	CREDIT
Checking	31,860.68	
Accounts Receivable	1,425.00	
Inventory Asset	5,410.00	
Prepaid Expenses	6,800.00	
Supplies Asset	450.00	
Undeposited Funds	925.00	
Furniture:Original Cost	4,875.00	
Machinery & Equipment:Depreciation		1,000.00
Machinery & Equipment:Original cost	10,000.00	
Investments	3,200.00	
Accounts Payable		8,670.00
AMEX		240.00
Payroll Tax Payable		2,484.94
Notes Payable		27,625.00
Common Stock		25,100.00
Opening Balance Equity		0.00
Retained Earnings		7,585.00
Sales		5,700.00
Services		225.00
Cost of Goods Sold	3,020.00	
Advertising	500.00	
Insurance	400.00	
Interest Expense	300.00	
Meals and Entertainment	240.00	
Payroll	9,224.26	
TOTAL	$78,629.94	$78,629.94

Figure 7.19

Trial Balance (as of 1/31/19)

8 Create and print a Transaction Report for the Checking account.

9 Create and print a Transaction Report for the Payroll Tax Payable account.

10 If your trial balance differs from the one in Figure 7.19, do the following:

a. Make sure all of your changes were dated in January 2019.

b. View the Transaction Reports you created to locate any errors.

c. Ask your instructor for assistance.

d. Be sure your company matches the above since, in the following chapter, you will add additional business events.

11 Export your Trial Balance report to Excel, and save it with the file name: Student Name (replace with your name) Ch 07 Case 02 Trial Balance.xlsx.

12 Open and print the custom report you created in the last chapter called Transaction Detail by Account.

13 Export your Transactions Detail by Account report to Excel, and save it with the file name: Student Name (replace with your name) Ch 07 Case 02 Transaction Detail by Account.xlsx.

14 Sign out of your company.

Case 3

Do not install QBO Payroll. Based on what you learned in the text, using the Sample Company, you are to add the following payroll-related activities to your company:

1 Add two new accounts like you did in the chapter: Payroll (expense) and Payroll Tax Payable (liability).

2 Add a new employee: Kira Jennings, 32 Ocean View Lane, La Jolla, CA, 92037, employee ID number: 556-33-3467.

3 Add a second employee: Jedi Vu, 2323 1ˢᵗ Street, La Jolla, CA, 92037, employee ID number: 458-22-1974.

4 Payroll is paid twice a month on the 16ᵗʰ and the last day of each month.

5 Record payroll (like you did in the chapter) for 1/16/20 based on the information shown in Figure 7.20 using checks 326 and 327. After recording each employee's check, be sure to designate it as a recurring transaction.

Figure 7.20

Payroll Information for 1/16/20

Pay/Tax/Withholding	Kira	Jedi	Total
Hours if applicable	n/a	70	
Annual salary or hourly rate	$ 48,000	$ 17.00	
Gross pay	**2,000.00**	**1,190.00**	**3,190.00**
Federal withholding	274.00	163.03	437.03
Social security employee (6.2%)	124.00	73.78	197.78
Medicare employee (1.45%)	29.00	17.26	46.26
Employee withholding	**427.00**	**254.07**	**681.07**
Social security employer (6.2%)	124.00	73.78	197.78
Medicare company employer (1.45%)	29.00	17.26	46.26
Employer payroll tax expense	**153.00**	**91.04**	**244.04**
Net Check amount	1,573.00	935.93	**2,508.93**

6 Use the recurring transactions template you created above to help you record payroll (like you did in the chapter) for 1/31/20 based on the information shown in Figure 7.21 using checks 328 and 329.

Pay/Tax/Withholding	Kira	Jedi	Total
Hours if applicable	n/a	75	
Annual salary or hourly rate	$ 48,000	$ 17.00	
Gross pay	**2,000.00**	**1,275.00**	**3,275.00**
Federal withholding	274.00	174.68	**448.68**
Social security employee (6.2%)	124.00	79.05	**203.05**
Medicare employee (1.45%)	29.00	18.49	**47.49**
Employee withholding	**427.00**	**272.22**	**699.22**
Social security employer (6.2%)	124.00	79.05	**203.05**
Medicare company employer (1.45%)	29.00	18.49	**47.49**
Employer payroll tax expense	**153.00**	**97.54**	**250.54**
Net Check amount	1,573.00	1,002.78	**2,575.78**

Figure 7.21

Payroll Information for 1/31/20

7 Open your previously customized report named Trial Balance 1/31/20. Your report should look like Figure 7.22.

Figure 7.22

Trial Balance as of 1/31/20

Case 3 - Student Name (ID number)

TRIAL BALANCE
As of January 31, 2020

	DEBIT	CREDIT
Checking	50,768.29	
Accounts Receivable (A/R)	2,610.00	
Inventory Asset	5,700.00	
Prepaid Expenses	6,050.00	
Supplies Asset	327.00	
Undeposited Funds	0.00	
Buildings:Original cost	31,800.00	
Machinery & Equipment:Depreciation		2,000.00
Machinery & Equipment:Original cost	18,000.00	
Investments	5,700.00	
Accounts Payable (A/P)		8,900.00
AMEX		123.00
Payroll Tax Payable		1,874.87
State Board of Equalization Payable		675.00
Notes Payable		63,800.00
Common Stock		40,000.00
Opening Balance Equity		0.00
Owner's Equity		10,075.00
Sales of Product Income		6,750.00
Services		240.00
Cost of Goods Sold	4,500.00	
Advertising	1,300.00	
Insurance	300.00	
Interest Expense	300.00	
Meals and Entertainment	123.00	
Payroll	6,959.58	
TOTAL	$134,437.87	$134,437.87

8 Create and print a Transaction Report for the Checking account.

9 Create and print a Transaction Report for the Payroll Tax Payable account.

10 If your trial balance is different than Figure 7.22:

    a. Make sure that all of your changes were dated in January 2019.

    b. View the Transaction Reports you just created to locate any errors.

    c. Ask your instructor for assistance.

    d. Be sure your company matches the above as in the following chapter you'll be adding additional business events.

11 Export your Trial Balance report to Excel and save it with the file name: Student Name (replace with your name) Ch 07 Case 03 Trial Balance.xlsx.

12 Open and print the customized report you created in the last chapter called Transaction Detail by Account.

13 Export your Transactions Detail by Account report to Excel and save it with the file name: Student Name (replace with your name) Ch 07 Case 03 Transaction Detail by Account.xlsx.

14 Sign out of your company.

Budgets and Bank Reconciliations

Student Learning Outcomes

Upon completion of this chapter, the student will be able to do the following:

- Add budget amounts to create a budget
- Create Profit and Loss budget reports
- Reconcile a checking account and print a reconciliation report

Overview

Intuit has provided a sample company online to provide new users a test drive of its QBO product. In this chapter, you will open this sample company and practice budget activities in QBO and reconcile a bank account. Budgets and bank reconciliations provide internal control over business activities. Significant deviations between actual and budget amounts could identify and help resolve problems. Unexplained differences identified in bank reconciliations can point to possible fraud or incompetency issues.

Remember, if you stop in the middle of this work none of your work will be saved. So, when you return, the same sample company, without your work, will appear. In some parts of the chapter, you will be asked to sign out of the Sample Company and then sign back in so the Sample Company is reset to its original state. In the end of chapter work, you will be asked to perform the same tasks completed on the Sample Company on your Student Company. That work, of course, will be saved.

Budget Creation

In this section, you will be establishing a Profit and Loss budget in QBO, which tracks amounts in income and expense accounts. QBO will interview you to determine budget amounts. You will be creating your budget from scratch since you have no historical amounts in QBO.

To create a Profit and Loss budget for the Sample Company, do the following:

1 Open your Internet browser.

2 Type **https://qbo.intuit.com/redir/testdrive** into your browser's address text box, and press [**Enter**] to view the Sample Company Home page.

3 Click the **Gear** icon, and select **Budgeting** shown in Figure 8.1.

Figure 8.1

Budgeting window (accessing the budgeting process)

4 Read page 1 of the Creating a budget instructions, and click **Next**.

5 Select the option button titled **No amounts. Create budget from scratch** shown in Figure 8.2.

Figure 8.2

Creating a budget from scratch

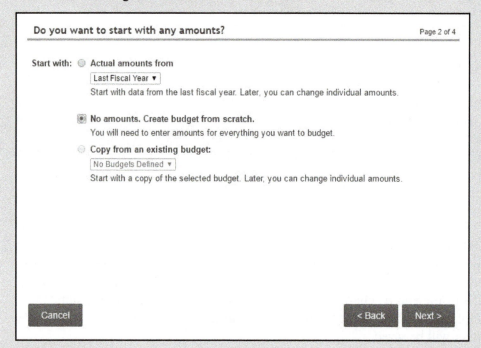

6 Click **Next**.

7 Select the option button titled **Don't subdivide**, and click **Next**.

8 Leave the default fiscal year provided, and type **Budget 1** as the Budget name. (The default fiscal year will change based on the date you use for the Sample Company. Thus, the dates in QBO will not match the dates shown in the text figures for the Sample Company.)

9 Click **Finish**. Then click **Finished**. Now click the **Gear** icon and then click **Budgeting**.

10 When the budget worksheet appears, click in the **Design income** account, which will activate the Edit – Design income section at the bottom of the worksheet.

11 Type **3,000** in the Jan: text box, then click the **Copy Across** button as shown in Figure 8.3.

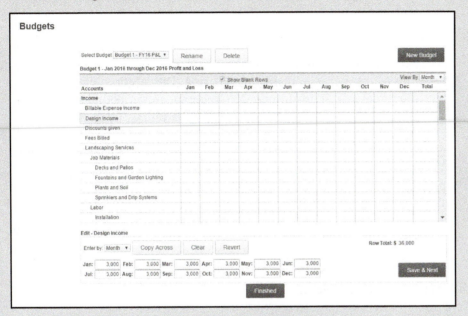

Figure 8.3

Profit and Loss (budget worksheet)

12 Click **Save & Next** to view Figure 8.4.

Figure 8.4

Profit and Loss (design income budget amounts)

13 Scroll down the budget worksheet as needed to enter the amounts shown in Figure 8.5.

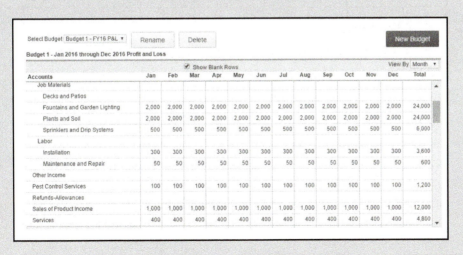

Figure 8.5

Profit and Loss (budget worksheet)

14 After entering the above amounts, click **Finished**. (This needs to be done even though you are not finished so QBO doesn't time out and make you start again.)

15 Click the **Gear** icon, and select **Budgeting** to continue the process.

16 Scroll down the budget worksheet, and add additional <u>monthly</u> amounts for cost of goods sold: **400**, advertising: **100**, automobile: **500**, equipment rental: **100**, insurance: **250**, job expenses: **1,000**, legal and professional: **950**, maintenance and repair: **900**, rent or lease: **800**, utilities: **500**, Miscellaneous: **3,000**.

17 Click **Finished**.

You have entered budgeted amounts and stored them in QBO. Now, view budget reports.

Budget Reports

QBO has two basic budget-related reports: Budget Overview and Budget vs. Actual. The overview report only lists budget data. The Budget vs. Actual lists budget data compared to actual transactions inputted into QBO.

To view budget reports in the Sample Company, do the following:

1 Continue from where you left off.

2 Click the **Reports**, type **Budget** in the Go to report text box.

3 Select **Budget Overview**, then click **Customize**, then click **Rows/Columns**, then select **Accounts vs. Total** from the Show Grid drop-down list, and then click **Run Report**. Now click **Collapse** to view the collapsed Budget Overview report for the year shown in Figure 8.6.

Craig's Design and Landscaping Services

BUDGET OVERVIEW: BUDGET 1 - FY16 P&L

January - December 2016

	TOTAL
▾ INCOME	
Design income	36,000.00
Landscaping Services	58,200.00
Pest Control Services	1,200.00
Sales of Product Income	12,000.00
Services	4,800.00
Total Income	**$112,200.00**
▾ COST OF GOODS SOLD	
Cost of Goods Sold	4,800.00
Total Cost of Goods Sold	**$4,800.00**
GROSS PROFIT	**$107,400.00**
▾ EXPENSES	
Advertising	1,200.00
Automobile	6,000.00
Equipment Rental	1,200.00
Insurance	3,000.00
Job Expenses	12,000.00
Legal & Professional Fees	11,400.00
Maintenance and Repair	10,800.00
Rent or Lease	9,600.00
Utilities	6,000.00
Total Expenses	**$61,200.00**
NET OPERATING INCOME	**$46,200.00**
▾ OTHER EXPENSES	
Miscellaneous	36,000.00
Total Other Expenses	**$36,000.00**
NET OTHER INCOME	**$ -36,000.00**
NET INCOME	**$10,200.00**

Figure 8.6

Budget Overview (collapsed report)

4 Click **Customize** to modify the Budget Overview report.

5 Change the From: and To: dates to the current month and year (In this case, the new From: is 11/1/16 and the new To: is 11/30/16. If your current system date, today's date, is, for example, 10/8/17, you would change the From: to 9/1/17 and the To: to 9/30/17.)

6 Check the **Without Cents** check box as shown in Figure 8.7.

Figure 8.7

Customizing Budget Overview

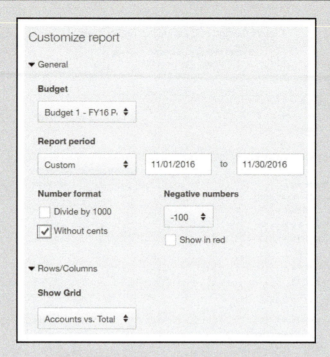

7   Click **Run Report** to view the customized Budget Overview report shown in Figure 8.8.

Figure 8.8

Budget Overview (customized report)

Craig's Design and Landscaping Services

BUDGET OVERVIEW: BUDGET 1 - FY16 P&L

November 2016

	TOTAL
▾ INCOME	
Design income	3,000
Landscaping Services	4,850
Pest Control Services	100
Sales of Product Income	1,000
Services	400
Total Income	**$9,350**
▾ COST OF GOODS SOLD	
Cost of Goods Sold	400
Total Cost of Goods Sold	**$400**
GROSS PROFIT	**$8,950**
▾ EXPENSES	
Advertising	100
Automobile	500
Equipment Rental	100
Insurance	250
Job Expenses	1,000
Legal & Professional Fees	950
Maintenance and Repair	900
Rent or Lease	800
Utilities	500
Total Expenses	**$5,100**
NET OPERATING INCOME	**$3,850**
▾ OTHER EXPENSES	
Miscellaneous	3,000
Total Other Expenses	**$3,000**
NET OTHER INCOME	$ -3,000
NET INCOME	$850

8   Click **Save Customizations**, type **Budget Overview** in the Name of custom report text box, then select **All** from the Share with drop-down list, and then click **Save**.

9   Click the **Reports**, Type **Budget** into the search text box, and then select **Budget vs. Actuals** from the list of recommended reports.

10   Click **Collapse**.

11   Click **Customize** to modify the Budget vs. Actuals report.

12   Change the From: and To: dates to the current previous month and year. (In this case, the new From: is 11/1/16 and the new To: is 11/30/16. If your current system date, today's date, is, for example, 10/8/17, you would change the From: to 9/1/17 and the To: to 9/30/17.)

13   Click **Rows/Columns** and then select **Accounts vs. Total** in the drop-down list in the Show Grid text box and then check the **Without Cents** check box as shown in Figure 8.9.

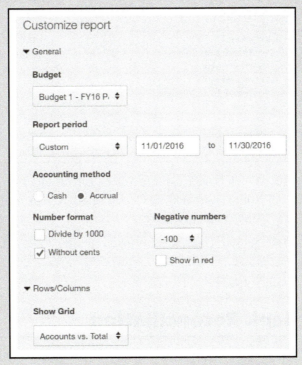

Figure 8.9

Customizing Budget vs. Actuals

14   Click **Run Report**. A partial view of the customized Budget vs. Actuals report is shown in Figure 8.10. Note: Your budget amounts should match this figure but your actual amounts will be different since the actual data changes based on when you are using the Sample Company.

Figure 8.10

Budget vs. Actual report

Craig's Design and Landscaping Services

BUDGET VS. ACTUALS: BUDGET 1 - FY16 P&L
November 2016

	ACTUAL	BUDGET	OVER BUDGET	% OF BUDGET
			TOTAL	
▾ INCOME				
Design income	1,275	3,000	-1,725	43.00 %
Discounts given	-59		-59	
Landscaping Services	2,039	4,850	-2,811	42.00 %
Pest Control Services	70	100	-30	70.00 %
Sales of Product Income	869	1,000	-131	87.00 %
Services	104	400	-296	26.00 %
Total Income	**$4,297**	**$9,350**	**$ -5,053**	**46.00 %**
▾ COST OF GOODS SOLD				
Cost of Goods Sold	405	400	5	101.00 %
Total Cost of Goods Sold	**$405**	**$400**	**$5**	**101.00 %**
GROSS PROFIT	$3,892	$8,950	$ -5,058	43.00 %
▾ EXPENSES				
Advertising	75	100	-25	75.00 %
Automobile	228	500	-272	46.00 %
Equipment Rental	112	100	12	112.00 %
Insurance	241	250	-9	96.00 %
Job Expenses	515	1,000	-485	51.00 %
Legal & Professional Fees	390	950	-560	41.00 %
Maintenance and Repair	940	900	40	104.00 %
Meals and Entertainment	23		23	
Office Expenses	18		18	
Rent or Lease		800	-800	
Utilities		500	-500	
Total Expenses	**$2,541**	**$5,100**	**$ -2,559**	**50.00 %**
NET OPERATING INCOME	$1,351	$3,850	$ -2,499	35.00 %

15 Click **Save Customizations,** type **Budget vs. Actuals** in the Name of custom report text box, then select **All** from the Share with drop-down list, and then click **Save**.

16 Sign out of the Sample Company.

Bank Reconciliation

Good internal control requires frequent reconciliations between bank records and a company's records of cash receipts and payments completed by someone other than the accountant or bookkeeper who is responsible for maintaining accounting records. The process involves comparing items that appear in the checking account with those items appearing on the bank statement. Deposits that appear in the checking account but do not appear on the bank statement are referred to as deposits in transit. Checks that appear in the checking account but do not appear on the bank statement are referred to as outstanding checks. They usually appear as checks on the next bank statement.

In QBO, if you discover a deposit recorded by the bank but not recorded in the checking account (determined to be an error in the checking account), you should correct the checking account by recording the deposit. Likewise, if you discover a check recorded by the bank but not recorded in the checking account (determined to be an error in the checking account), you should correct the checking account by recording the check. In the following example, neither was identified.

To create reconciliation for the Sample Company, do the following:

1 Open your Internet browser.

2 Type **https://qbo.intuit.com/redir/testdrive** into your browser's address text box, and press [**Enter**] to view the Sample Company Home page.

3 Click the **Gear** icon, and select **Reconcile** as shown in Figure 8.11.

Figure 8.11

Reconciliation process (access)

4 Make sure the **Checking** account is selected in the Reconcile window shown in Figure 8.12.

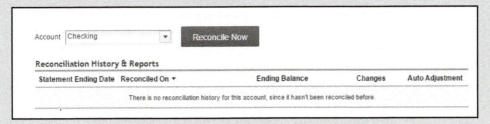

Figure 8.12

Reconcile window

5 Click **Reconcile Now**.

6 Type **11/30/16** as the Statement Ending Date, and type **1,026.41** as the Ending Balance. Your date will differ depending on your current system date. Usually, you will need to input the last day of the month from the month prior to your current system date.

7 Click **OK** to view the Reconcile – Checking form shown in Figure 8.13.

Figure 8.13

Reconcile - Checking form

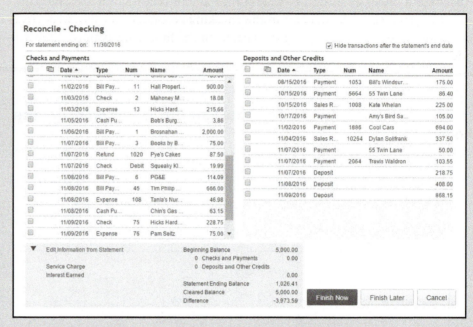

8 After a review of the company's most recent bank statement and a comparison with the company's checking account, you discover some checks and payments recorded in the checking account that did not appear on the bank statement. Place a check next to all checks and payments except for check **13** to Hicks Hardware for 215.66, check **75** to Hicks Hardware for 228.75, and check **76** to Pam Seitz for 75.00, none of which had cleared the bank.

9 After a review of the company's most recent bank statement and a comparison with the company's checking account, you discover some deposits and other credits recorded in the checking account that did not appear on the bank statement. Place a check next to all deposits and other credits <u>except</u> for payment **1886** from Cool Cars for 694.00 which had not cleared the bank.

10 Your account is reconciled as shown by the 0.00 difference between the Statement Ending Balance and the Cleared Balance shown in Figure 8.14. Be sure all the items referenced in the above steps (checks and payments as well as deposits and other credits) are properly checked or unchecked.

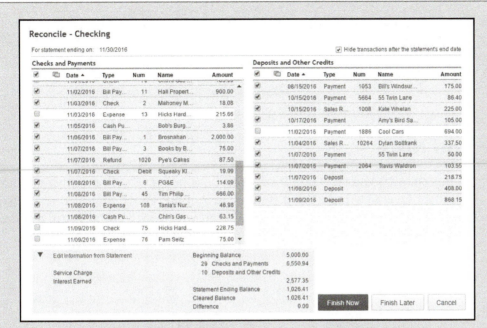

Figure 8.14

Reconcile – Checking form (reconciled account)

11 Once you have reconciled the checking account, click **Finish Now**.

12 A summary of all reconciliation reports completed should appear shown in Figure 8.15.

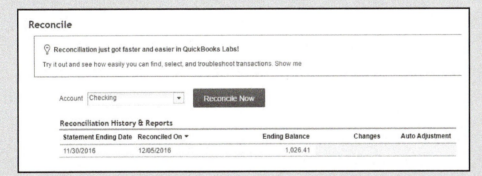

Figure 8.15

Reconcile (reconciliation summary)

13 Click on the reconciliation ending balance **1,026.41** to view the reconciliation report. The upper summary portion of that report is shown in Figure 8.16.

Figure 8.16

Summary Reconciliation Report

14 Click **Print**, click **OK**, and click **Close** to print the report and close its window.

15 Sign out of the Sample Company.

End Note

In this chapter, you created a Profit and Loss budget for 12 months, prepared a Budget Overview report and Budget vs. Actual report, and reconciled your checking account. In the next chapter, you will work with adjusting journal entries.

Chapter 8 Questions

1 What are the steps to create a Profit and Loss budget?

2 What value do budgets provide a business?

3 Why should a business reconcile a checking account?

4 Who should prepare a bank reconciliation?

5 What options are available when creating a budget other than creating one from scratch?

6 What button is used to replicate amounts across several months in the budget worksheet?

7 How do you know if you have correctly reconciled an account?

8 What are the steps to change a Budget Overview report from covering a year to covering just one month?

9 What should you do if you discover a deposit was recorded by the bank but not recorded in the checking account (determined to be an error in the checking account)?

10 What are the steps to print a bank reconciliation report?

Chapter 8 Matching

a. Budget Overview report   _____ Condenses a report

b. Budget vs. Actual report   _____ Do not appear on the bank statement

c. Deposits in transit   _____ Used to change report dates

d. Outstanding checks   _____ Includes only budget amounts

e. Collapse   _____ Usually appear as checks on the next bank statement

f. Customize   _____ Includes both budget and actual amounts

Chapter 8 Cases

The following cases require you to open the company you updated in Chapter 7. Each of the following cases continues throughout the text in a sequential manner. For example, if you are assigned Case 01, you will use the file you modified in this chapter in all following chapters. Each of the following cases is similar in concepts assessed but differs in amounts and transactions.

To reopen your company, do the following:

1 Open your Internet browser.

2 Type **https://qbo.intuit.com/qbo28/loginwebredir** into your browser's address text box.

3 Type your User ID and Password into the text boxes as you have done before.

Case 1

Based on what you learned in the text, using the Sample Company, you are to add the following activities to your company:

1. Add an invoice on 1/30/18 to customer: Blondie's Boards, terms: Net 30, for 4 Fred Rubbles, 7 Water Hogs, and 8 Rook 15 surfboards.

2. Add an invoice on 1/31/18 to a new customer: Surf Rider Foundation, terms: Net 30, for 100 hours of consulting.

3. Add the following FY 2018 (Jan 2018 – Dec 2018) <u>monthly</u> budgeted amounts as you did earlier in the chapter: sales: 40,000, services: 3,000, cost of goods sold: 23,500, interest expense: 600, payroll: 12,000, rent or lease: 2500, travel: 500, utilities: 200. Amounts provided should be input for each month of 2018. Use Budget 1 as the budget name.

4. Create and customize, save customization as Budget Overview Budget 1, print, and export to Excel a Budget Overview report for the month of January 2018. Your report should look like Figure 8.17.

Figure 8.17

Budget Overview (January 2018)

Case 1
BUDGET OVERVIEW: BUDGET 1 - FY18 P&L
January 2018

	TOTAL
Income	
Sales	40,000.00
Services	3,000.00
Total Income	**$43,000.00**
Cost of Goods Sold	
Cost of Goods Sold	23,500.00
Total Cost of Goods Sold	**$23,500.00**
Gross Profit	**$19,500.00**
Expenses	
Interest Expense	600.00
Payroll	12,000.00
Rent or Lease	2,500.00
Travel	500.00
Utilities	200.00
Total Expenses	**$15,800.00**
Net Operating Income	**$3,700.00**
Net Income	**$3,700.00**

5. Create and customize, save customization as Budget vs. Actual Budget 1, print, and export to Excel a Budget vs. Actuals report for the month of January 2018. Your report should look like Figure 8.18.

Figure 8.18

Budget vs. Actuals (January 2018)

Case 1
BUDGET VS. ACTUALS: BUDGET 1 - FY18 P&L
January 2018

	ACTUAL	BUDGET	OVER BUDGET	% OF BUDGET
Income				
Sales	17,180.00	40,000.00	-22,820.00	42.95 %
Services	2,670.00	3,000.00	-330.00	89.00 %
Total Income	**$19,850.00**	**$43,000.00**	**$ -23,150.00**	**46.16 %**
Cost of Goods Sold				
Cost of Goods Sold	10,400.00	23,500.00	-13,100.00	44.26 %
Total Cost of Goods Sold	**$10,400.00**	**$23,500.00**	**$ -13,100.00**	**44.26 %**
Gross Profit	**$9,450.00**	**$19,500.00**	**$ -10,050.00**	**48.46 %**
Expenses				
Interest Expense	600.00	600.00	0.00	100.00 %
Payroll	11,785.71	12,000.00	-214.29	98.21 %
Rent or Lease	2,500.00	2,500.00	0.00	100.00 %
Travel	1,800.00	500.00	1,300.00	360.00 %
Utilities	145.00	200.00	-55.00	72.50 %
Total Expenses	**$16,830.71**	**$15,800.00**	**$1,030.71**	**106.52 %**
Net Operating Income	**$ -7,380.71**	**$3,700.00**	**$ -11,080.71**	**-199.48 %**
Net Income	**$ -7,380.71**	**$3,700.00**	**$ -11,080.71**	**-199.48 %**

6 Open and print the custom report you created in the last chapter called Transaction Detail by Account.

7 Export your Transactions Detail by Account report to Excel and save it with the file name: Student Name (replace with your name) Ch 08 Case 01 Transaction Detail by Account.xlsx.

8 Reconcile your company's checking account. No services charges were incurred or interest earned. The ending bank statement balance on 1/31/18 was $29,202.37.

9 After a review of the company's most recent bank statement and a comparison with the company's checking account, you discover some checks and payments recorded in the checking account that did not appear on the bank statement. Place a check next to all checks and payments except for check 1009 to Ben Franklin for 3,113.22 and check 1010 to Betsy Ross for 1,149.87, neither of which had cleared the bank.

10 After a review of the company's most recent bank statement and a comparison with the company's checking account, you discover some deposits and other credits recorded in the checking account that did not appear on the bank statement. Place a check next to all deposits and other credits except for a deposit on 1/8/18 from Blondie's Boards for 1,300.00, which had not cleared the bank.

11 Print the resulting Reconciliation Report.

12 Sign out of your company.

Case 2

Based on what you learned in the text and using the Sample Company, you are to add the following activities to your company:

1   Add an invoice on 1/30/19 to customer: Hagen's Toys, terms: Net 30, for 100 hours of custom painting.

2   Add an invoice on 1/31/19 to a new customer: Zack's RC, terms: Net 30, for 2 Seawind Carbon Sailboats and 2 Mystique RES.

3   Add the following FY 2019 (Jan 2019 – Dec 2019) <u>monthly</u> budgeted amounts like you did in the chapter: sales: 10,000, services: 4,000, cost of goods sold: 5,000, advertising: 500, insurance: 425, interest expense: 300, meals and entertainment: 250, and payroll: 9,000. Amounts provided should be input for each month of 2019. Use Budget 1 as the budget name.

4   Create and customize, save customization as Budget Overview Budget 1, print, and export to Excel a Budget Overview report for the month of January 2019. Your report should look like Figure 8.19.

Figure 8.19

Budget Overview (January 2019)

Case 2
BUDGET OVERVIEW: BUDGET 1 - FY19 P&L
January 2019

	TOTAL
Income	
Sales	10,000.00
Services	4,000.00
Total Income	$14,000.00
Cost of Goods Sold	
Cost of Goods Sold	5,000.00
Total Cost of Goods Sold	$5,000.00
Gross Profit	$9,000.00
Expenses	
Advertising	500.00
Insurance	425.00
Interest Expense	300.00
Meals and Entertainment	250.00
Payroll	9,000.00
Total Expenses	$10,475.00
Net Operating Income	$ -1,475.00
Net Income	$ -1,475.00

5   Create and customize, save customization as Budget vs. Actuals Budget 1, print, and export to Excel a Budget vs. Actuals report for the month of January 2019. Your report should look like Figure 8.20.

Figure 8.20

Budget vs. Actuals (January 2019)

Case 2
BUDGET VS. ACTUALS: BUDGET 1 - FY19 P&L
January 2019

	ACTUAL	BUDGET	OVER BUDGET	% OF BUDGET
Income				
Sales	9,000.00	10,000.00	−1,000.00	90.00 %
Services	4,725.00	4,000.00	725.00	118.13 %
Total Income	**$13,725.00**	**$14,000.00**	**$ −275.00**	**98.04 %**
Cost of Goods Sold				
Cost of Goods Sold	4,910.00	5,000.00	−90.00	98.20 %
Total Cost of Goods Sold	**$4,910.00**	**$5,000.00**	**$ -90.00**	**98.20 %**
Gross Profit	**$8,815.00**	**$9,000.00**	**$ −185.00**	**97.94 %**
Expenses				
Advertising	500.00	500.00	0.00	100.00 %
Insurance	400.00	425.00	−25.00	94.12 %
Interest Expense	300.00	300.00	0.00	100.00 %
Meals and Entertainment	240.00	250.00	−10.00	96.00 %
Payroll	9,224.26	9,000.00	224.26	102.49 %
Total Expenses	**$10,664.26**	**$10,475.00**	**$189.26**	**101.81 %**
Net Operating Income	**$ −1,849.26**	**$ −1,475.00**	**$ −374.26**	**125.37 %**
Net Income	**$ −1,849.26**	**$ −1,475.00**	**$ −374.26**	**125.37 %**

6 Open and print the custom report you created in the last chapter called Transaction Detail by Account.

7 Export your Transactions Detail by Account report to Excel and save it with the file name: Student Name (replace with your name) Ch 08 Case 02 Transaction Detail by Account.xlsx.

8 Reconcile your company's checking account. No service charges were incurred or interest earned. The ending bank statement balance on 1/31/19 was $30,693.47.

9 After a review of the company's most recent bank statement and a comparison with the company's checking account, you discover some checks and payments recorded in the checking account that did not appear on the bank statement. Place a check next to all checks and payments <u>except</u> for check 1009 to Frank Benjamin for 2,359.50 and check 1010 to Sara Juarez for 973.29, neither of which had cleared the bank.

10 After a review of the company's most recent bank statement and a comparison with the company's checking account, you discover a deposit and other credit recorded in the checking account that did not appear on the bank statement. Place a check next to all deposits and other credits <u>except</u> for a deposit on 1/7/19 from Benson's RC for 4,500.00, which had not cleared the bank.

11 Print the resulting Reconciliation Report.

12 Sign out of your company.

Case 3

Based on what you learned in the text, using the Sample Company, you are to add the following activities to your company:

1 Add the following bill and product received from Samsung, Inc. on 1/30/20, terms: Net 15, received 5 Samsung Galaxy 8 and 8 Samsung Note phones.

2 Add an invoice on 1/30/20 to a new taxable customer: Diamond Girl, Inc., terms: Net 30, for 4 Samsung Galaxy 8 and 5 Samsung Note phones and 6 hours of Phone Consulting.

3 Add a payment received from GHO Marketing on 1/31/20 for $2,610, which was deposited the same day into the checking account.

4 Add the following FY 2020 (Jan 2020 – Dec 2020) <u>monthly</u> budgeted amounts like you did in the chapter: sales of product income: 20,000, services: 1,000, cost of goods sold: 10,000, advertising: 1,000, insurance: 500, interest expense: 350, meals and entertainment: 250, and payroll: 7,000. Amounts provided should be input for each month of 2020. Use Budget 2 as the budget name.

5 Create and customize a Budget Overview report for January 2020 with no cents. Save customization as Budget Overview Budget 2, print, and export to Excel a Budget Overview report for the month of January 2020. Your report should look like Figure 8.21.

Figure 8.21

Budget Overview for January 2020

Case 3 - Student Name (ID number)

BUDGET OVERVIEW: BUDGET 2 - FY20 P&L

January 2020

	TOTAL
▾ INCOME	
Sales of Product Income	20,000
Services	1,000
Total Income	**$21,000**
▾ COST OF GOODS SOLD	
Cost of Goods Sold	10,000
Total Cost of Goods Sold	**$10,000**
GROSS PROFIT	**$11,000**
▾ EXPENSES	
Advertising	1,000
Insurance	500
Interest Expense	350
Meals and Entertainment	250
Payroll	7,000
Total Expenses	**$9,100**
NET OPERATING INCOME	**$1,900**
NET INCOME	**$1,900**

6 Create and customize, save customization as Budget vs. Actuals Budget 2, print, and export to Excel a Budget vs. Actuals report for the month of January 2020. Your report should look like Figure 8.22.

Case 3 - Student Name (ID number)

BUDGET VS. ACTUALS: BUDGET 2 - FY20 P&L

January 2020

	TOTAL			
	ACTUAL	BUDGET	OVER BUDGET	% OF BUDGET
▾ INCOME				
Sales of Product Income	12,800	20,000	-7,200	64.00 %
Services	450	1,000	-550	45.00 %
Total Income	**$13,250**	**$21,000**	**$ -7,750**	**63.00 %**
▾ COST OF GOODS SOLD				
Cost of Goods Sold	9,150	10,000	-850	92.00 %
Total Cost of Goods Sold	**$9,150**	**$10,000**	**$ -850**	**92.00 %**
GROSS PROFIT	**$4,100**	**$11,000**	**$ -6,900**	**37.00 %**
▾ EXPENSES				
Advertising	1,300	1,000	300	130.00 %
Insurance	300	500	-200	60.00 %
Interest Expense	300	350	-50	86.00 %
Meals and Entertainment	123	250	-127	49.00 %
Payroll	6,960	7,000	-40	99.00 %
Total Expenses	**$8,983**	**$9,100**	**$ -117**	**99.00 %**
NET OPERATING INCOME	**$ -4,883**	**$1,900**	**$ -6,783**	**-257.00 %**
NET INCOME	**$ -4,883**	**$1,900**	**$ -6,783**	**-257.00 %**

Figure 8.22

Budget vs. Actuals for January 2020

7 Reconcile your company's checking account. No service charges were incurred or interest earned. The ending bank statement balance on 1/31/20 was $51,771.07.

8 After a review of the company's most recent statement and a comparison with the company's checking account you note that 1 check and 1 deposit that were recorded in the checking account did not appear on the bank statement. Place a check next to all checks and payments <u>except</u> for check 329 to Jedi Vu for 1,002.78 and the deposit from GHO Marketing for 2,610.00, which had not cleared the bank.

9 Print the resulting Reconciliation Report.

10 Sign out of your company.

Adjusting Entries

Upon completion of this chapter, the student will be able to do the following:

- Prepare an unadjusted trial balance
- Make adjusting entries for the following:
    - o Prepaid expenses
    - o Accrued expenses
    - o Unearned revenue
    - o Accrued revenue
    - o Depreciation

Overview

Intuit has provided a Sample Company online to let new users test drive its QBO product. In this chapter, you will open this Sample Company and practice adjusting entry activities in QBO. Prior to the creation of periodic financial statements, generally accepted accounting principles (GAAP) require that accounting records be adjusted to reflect accrual accounting. This process insures revenues are recorded in the period in which they are earned and that expenses are recorded in the period in which they were consumed. In the process, expenses will be matched in the same period to the revenues generated from incurring those expenses.

There are five types of adjusting entries. Expenses paid, prior to being consumed, should be deferred (such as supplies, rent, insurance, etc.) and recorded as assets (such as supplies asset, prepaid rent, prepaid insurance, etc.) until they are consumed. To defer is to postpone. Expenses incurred prior to being paid (payroll, rent, utilities, etc.) must be recorded and accrued as a liability. To accrue is to increase. Revenue collected prior to being earned must be deferred (such as sales, services, etc.) and recorded as liabilities (such as unearned revenue) until they are earned. Revenues earned prior to being collected (sales and services, etc.) must be recorded and accrued as a receivable. Lastly, fixed assets (buildings, furniture, equipment, vehicles, etc.) must be depreciated over their useful life to match costs with revenues.

Remember, if you stop in the middle of this work, none of your work will be saved. So, when you return, the same sample company, without your work, will appear. In some parts of the chapter, you will be asked to sign out of the Sample Company and sign back in so the Sample Company is reset to its original state. In the end of chapter work, you will be asked to perform the same tasks

completed on the Sample Company on your Student Company. That work, of course, will be saved.

Trial Balance

In this section, you will create a trial balance (before adjusting entries), which must be analyzed in light of end of the period business events to determine the required adjusting entries.

To create a trial balance for the Sample Company, do the following:

1 Open your Internet browser.

2 Type **https://qbo.intuit.com/redir/testdrive** into your browser's address text box and the press [**Enter**] to view the Sample Company Home page.

3 Click **Reports** from the navigation bar.

4 Type **Trial Balance** in the Go to report search box and the press [**Enter**].

5 Change the From: date to the first of the previous month and the To: date to the last day of the previous month (in this case **11/1/16** and **11/30/16**; your date will be different), then click **Run Report** to view the trial balance shown in Figure 9.1.

Figure 9.1

Trial Balance report (partial view)

Craig's Design and Landscaping Services

TRIAL BALANCE
As of November 30, 2016

	DEBIT	CREDIT
Checking	1,201.00	
Savings	800.00	
Accounts Receivable (A/R)	5,281.52	
Inventory Asset	596.25	
Undeposited Funds	2,062.52	
Truck:Original Cost	13,495.00	
Accounts Payable (A/P)		1,602.67
Mastercard		123.72
Arizona Dept. of Revenue Payable		0.00
Board of Equalization Payable		370.94
Loan Payable		4,000.00
Notes Payable		25,000.00
Opening Balance Equity	9,337.50	
Design income		2,250.00
Discounts given	89.50	
Landscaping Services		1,477.50
Landscaping Services:Job Materials:Fountains and Garden Lighting		2,246.50
Landscaping Services:Job Materials:Plants and Soil		2,351.97
Landscaping Services:Job Materials:Sprinklers and Drip Systems		138.00
Landscaping Services:Labor:Installation		250.00
Landscaping Services:Labor:Maintenance and Repair		50.00
Pest Control Services		110.00
Sales of Product Income		912.75
Services		503.55
Cost of Goods Sold	405.00	

Adjusting Journal Entries: Prepaid Expenses

Further investigation of this trial balance and period end business activities indicates that $500 of supplies were recorded as a miscellaneous expense but should have been deferred as a supplies asset until consumed in some future period. Thus, an adjusting entry is necessary.

To record an adjusting entry for supplies in the Sample Company, do the following:

1   Continue from where you left off. If you closed the Sample Company, follow the steps to reopen it found at the beginning of this chapter.

2   Click the **Create** (+) icon, and click **Journal Entry**.

3   Type the last day of the previous month into the **Journal date** text box (in this case 11/30/16).

4   Type **Supplies Asset** on line 1 of the Account column, and click **+ Add Supplies Asset** shown in Figure 9.2. (This is another way to add a new account in QBO.)

Figure 9.2

Journal entry (adding a new account)

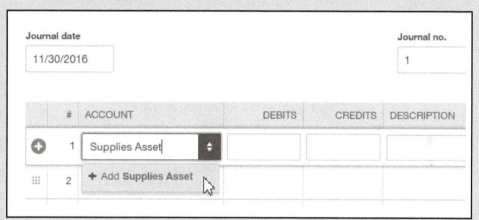

5   Select **Other Current Assets** from the drop-down list in the **Category Type** text box.

6   Select **Prepaid Expenses** from the drop-down list in the **Detail Type** text box.

7   Click **Save and Close**.

8   Type **500** into the Debit column of line 1.

9   Select **Miscellaneous** from the drop-down list in line 2 of the Accounts column.

10 Accept **500** into the Credit column of line 2 to view the journal entry shown in Figure 9.3.

Figure 9.3

Journal Entry #1 (to defer supplies)

11 Click **Save and Close**.

The same process could be used to defer a cost that had been recorded as an expense but should be deferred as an asset at period end. Examples might include insurance to be deferred as either prepaid insurance or prepaid expenses or as rent be deferred as either prepaid rent or prepaid expenses.

Another example of this occurs when an expense is deferred in a prior period but is consumed in the current period. We will use the Supplies Asset created as an example assuming $100 of supplies were consumed in the month leaving $400 of supplies as an asset.

To record an adjusting journal entry to record the consumption of supplies, do the following:

1 Continue from where you left off. If you closed the Sample Company, follow the steps to reopen it found at the beginning of this chapter.

2 Click the **Create +** icon and then click **Journal Entry**.

3 Type the last day of the previous month into the **Journal date** text box (in this case 11/30/16).

4 Select **Supplies** from the drop-down list in line 1 of the Account column. (This is an expense account already in the Company's chart of accounts.)

5 Type **100** into the Debit column of line 1.

6 Select **Supplies Asset** from the drop-down list in line 2 of the Accounts column.

7 Accept **100** into the Credit column of line 2 to view the journal entry shown in Figure 9.4.

Figure 9.4

Journal entry (recording the consumption of supplies)

Journal date				Journal no.	
11/30/2016				2	

	#	ACCOUNT	DEBITS	CREDITS	DESCRIPTION
⠿	1	Supplies	100.00		
⠿	2	Supplies Asset		100.00	

8 Click **Save and Close**.

9 Closing the journal entry should reveal the trial balance created before but updated to reflect the supplies asset account shown in Figure 9.5.

Figure 9.5

Trial Balance after supplies adjustments (partial view)

Craig's Design and Landscaping Services

TRIAL BALANCE
As of November 30, 2016

	DEBIT	CREDIT
Checking	1,201.00	
Savings	800.00	
Accounts Receivable (A/R)	5,281.52	
Inventory Asset	596.25	
Supplies Asset	400.00	
Undeposited Funds	2,062.52	
Truck:Original Cost	13,495.00	

10 Click the Supplies Asset **400.00** amount to reveal a Transaction Report for the Supplies Asset account shown in Figure 9.6.

11 Click **Back to Summary Report** to return to the Trial Balance report.

Figure 9.6

Transaction Report (for supplies asset)

The first entry deferred $500 from miscellaneous expense; the second entry recorded the consumption of supplies reducing the asset account.

Adjusting Journal Entries: Accrued Expenses

Further investigation of this trial balance and period end business activities indicates that a bill for $300 was received and recorded in the next month for advertising consumed in the current month. Thus, an adjusting journal entry needs to be made to accrue this expense. For our purposes, we will create a new accrued liabilities account to keep track of these accruals and keep them separate from accounts payable.

To record an adjusting journal entry to record the accrual of advertising expense, do the following:

1 Continue from where you left off. If you closed the Sample Company, follow the steps to reopen it found at the beginning of this chapter.

2 Click the **Create +** icon, and click **Journal Entry**.

3 Type the last day of the previous month into the Journal date text box (in this case 11/30/16).

4 Select **Advertising** from the drop-down list in line 1 of the Account column.

5 Type **300** into the Debits column of line 1.

6 Type **Accrued Liabilities** on line 2 of the Account column and then click **+ Add Accrued Liabilities**.

7 Select **Other Current Liabilities** from the drop-down list in the **Category Type** text box.

8 Select **Other Current Liabilities** from the drop-down list in the **Detail Type** text box.

9   Click **Save and Close**.

10   Accept **300** into the Credits column of line 2 to view the journal entry shown in Figure 9.7.

Figure 9.7

Journal entry (accruing advertising expense)

11   Click **Save and Close**.

12   Closing the journal entry should reveal the trial balance created before but now updated to reflect the accrual of advertising expense to the accrued liabilities account.

13   Click the Accrued Liabilities **300.00** amount to reveal a Transaction Report.

14   Click **Back to Summary Report** to return to the Trial Balance report.

Adjusting Journal Entries: Unearned Revenue

Further investigation of this trial balance and period end business activities indicates that design income recorded on sales receipt #1003 for $337.50 to Dylan Sollfrank were never performed even though cash had been received. Thus, the revenue had not been earned. Work is expected to occur next month, thus this amount of revenue must be deferred and set up as an unearned revenue liability.

To record an adjusting journal entry to reflect earned revenue, do the following:

1   Continue from where you left off. If you closed the Sample Company, follow the steps to reopen it found at the beginning of this chapter.

2   Click the **Create +** icon and then click **Journal Entry**.

3   Type the last day of the previous month into the Journal date text box (in this case 11/30/16).

4   Select **Design Income** from the drop-down list in line 1 of the Account column.

5   Type **337.50** into the Debits column of line **1**.

6   Select **Dylan Sollfrank** from the drop-down list of customers in the Name column of line 1.

7   Type **Unearned Revenue** on line 2 of the Account column and then click **+ Add Unearned Revenue**.

8   Select **Other Current Liabilities** from the drop-down list in the **Category Type** text box.

9   Select **Other Current Liabilities** from the drop-down list in the **Detail Type** text box.

10   Click **Save and Close**.

11   Accept **337.50** into the Credits column of line 2 to view the journal entry shown in Figure 9.8.

12   Click **Save and Close**.

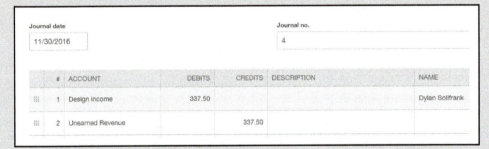

Figure 9.8

Journal entry (recording unearned revenue)

13   Closing the journal entry should reveal the trial balance created before but updated to reflect the deferral of revenue to the unearned revenue liability account.

14   Click the Unearned Revenue **337.50** amount to reveal a Transaction Report.

15   Click **Back to Summary Report** to return to the Trial Balance report.

Adjusting Journal Entries: Accruing Revenue

Further investigation of this trial balance and period end business activities indicates that some landscaping services of $500 were performed on the last day of the month for Diego Rodriguez but not invoiced to the customer or recorded into the accounting records until a few days into the next month. Thus, you will need to record an adjusting journal entry to accrue revenue and an accrued receivable.

To record an adjusting journal entry to reflect earned revenue, do the following:

1 Continue from where you left off. If you closed the Sample Company, follow the steps to reopen it found at the beginning of this chapter.

2 Click the **Create +** icon and then click **Journal Entry**.

3 Type the last day of the previous month into the **Journal date** text box (in this case 11/30/16).

4 Type **Accrued Receivable** on line 1 of the Account column and then click **+ Add Accrued Receivable**.

5 Select **Other Current Assets** from the drop-down list in the **Category Type** text box.

6 Select **Other Current Assets** from the drop-down list in the **Detail Type** text box.

7 Click **Save and Close**.

8 Type **500** into the Debits column of line 1.

9 Select **Diego Rodriguez** from the drop-down list of customers in the Name column of line 1.

10 Select **Landscaping Services** from the drop-down list in line 2 of the Account column.

11 Accept **500** in the Credits column of line 2.

12 Select **Diego Rodriguez** from the drop-down list of customers in the Name column of line 2 to view the journal entry shown in Figure 9.9.

Figure 9.9

Journal entry (recording accrued revenue)

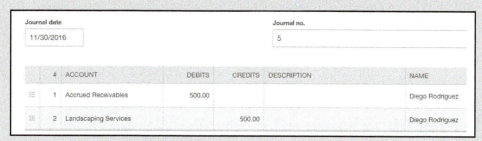

Journal date					Journal no.	
11/30/2016					5	

	#	ACCOUNT	DEBITS	CREDITS	DESCRIPTION	NAME
⠿	1	Accrued Receivables	500.00			Diego Rodriguez
⠿	2	Landscaping Services		500.00		Diego Rodriguez

13 Click **Save and Close**.

14 Closing the journal entry should reveal the trial balance created before but updated to reflect the accrual of revenue to the accrued receivable account.

15 Click the Accrued Receivable **500.00** amount to reveal a Transaction Report.

16 Click **Back to Summary Report** to return to the Trial Balance report.

Adjusting Journal Entries: Depreciation

Further investigation of this trial balance and period end business activities indicates the company's only fixed asset, a truck, needed to be depreciated for the month. Monthly depreciation is $1,000. Normally, the adjusting entry would

debit depreciation expense and credit accumulated depreciation. However, the accounts set up in the Sample Company are both named depreciation. Thus, you decide to change the account names first and then record the depreciation adjusting journal entry.

To edit account names and then record an adjusting journal entry to record depreciation, do the following:

1 Continue from where you left off. If you closed the Sample Company, follow the steps to reopen it found at the beginning of this chapter.

2 Click the **Gear** icon and then click **Chart of Accounts**.

3 Click **Edit** from the drop-down arrow next to the words View Register on the Depreciation line listed under the Truck account.

4 Type **Accumulated** <u>in front</u> of Depreciation in the **Name** text box and then click **Save and Close**.

5 Scroll down to the bottom of the chart of accounts and select **Edit** from the drop-down arrow next to the words Run report on the Depreciation line listed above Miscellaneous.

6 Type **Expense** <u>after</u> Depreciation in the **Name** text box and then click **Save and Close**.

7 Click the **Create +** icon and then click **Journal Entry**.

8 Type the last day of the previous month into the Journal date text box (in this case 11/30/16).

9 Select **Depreciation Expense** from the drop-down list in line 1 of the Account column.

10 Type **1,000** into the Debits column of line 1.

11 Select **Truck:Accumulated Depreciation** from the drop-down list in line 2 of the Accounts column.

12 Accept **1,000.00** as the Credits column amount. Your screen should look like Figure 9.10.

	Journal date			Journal no.	
	11/30/2016			6	

	#	ACCOUNT	DEBITS	CREDITS	DESCRIPTION
⠿	1	Depreciation Expense	1,000.00		
⠿	2	Truck:Accumulated Depreciation		1,000.00	

Figure 9.10

Journal entry (recording depreciation)

13 Click **Save and Close**.

14 Click **Reports** from the navigation bar and then type **Trial Balance** in the **Go to report** text box and then press [**Enter**] to view the trial balance.

15 Change the To: and From: dates like you did earlier in this chapter to reveal a trial balance now updated to reflect the depreciation expense and accumulated depreciation just recorded.

16 Click the Truck:Accumulated Depreciation **1,000.00** amount to reveal a Transaction Report.

17 Click **Back to Summary Report** to return to the Trial Balance report. Your completed Trial Balance report should look like Figure 9.11.

Figure 9.11

Revised Trial Balance report (partial view)

Craig's Design and Landscaping Services

TRIAL BALANCE
As of November 30, 2016

	DEBIT	CREDIT
Checking	1,201.00	
Savings	800.00	
Accounts Receivable (A/R)	5,281.52	
Accrued Receivables	500.00	
Inventory Asset	596.25	
Supplies Asset	400.00	
Undeposited Funds	2,062.52	
Truck:Accumulated Depreciation		1,000.00
Truck:Original Cost	13,495.00	
Accounts Payable (A/P)		1,602.67
Mastercard		123.72
Accrued Liabilities		300.00
Arizona Dept. of Revenue Payable		0.00
Board of Equalization Payable		370.94
Loan Payable		4,000.00
Unearned Revenue		337.50
Notes Payable		25,000.00
Opening Balance Equity	9,337.50	

End Note

In this chapter, you recorded adjusting entries to create accrual accounting based records. In the next chapter, you will create financial statements and useful reports.

Chapter 9 Questions

1 What is an unadjusted trial balance?

2 What is an adjusted trial balance?

3 Why accrue an expense?

4 Why defer an expense?

5 Why accrue revenues?

6 Why defer revenues?

7 What QBO task is used to record accruals and deferrals?

8 Why depreciate a fixed asset?

9 Describe the new method you learned in this chapter to add a new account from within a journal entry.

10 Describe the new method you learned in this chapter to add a new customer or vendor from within a journal entry.

Chapter 9 Matching

a. Prepaid Expenses

b. Accrued Expenses

c. Unearned Revenue

d. Accrued Revenue

e. Depreciation Expense

f. Supplies Asset

g. Supplies Expense

h. Accrued Receivables

i. Accrued Liabilities

j. Accumulate Depreciation

_____ Debit this account when recording depreciation

_____ Credit this account when accruing an expense

_____ Debit this account when accruing revenue

_____ Supplies consumed

_____ Credit this account when recording depreciation

_____ Expenses not yet consumed

_____ Revenue not yet earned

_____ To increase

_____ Supplies not yet consumed

_____ To postpone

Chapter 9 Cases

The following cases require you to open the company you updated in Chapter 8. Each of the following cases continues throughout the text in a sequential manner. For example, if you are assigned Case 1, you will use the file you modified in this chapter in all following chapters. Each of the following cases is similar in concepts assessed but differs in amounts and transactions.

To reopen your company, do the following:

1 Open your Internet browser.

2 Type **https://qbo.intuit.com/qbo28/login?webredir** into your browser's address text box.

3 Type your User ID and Password into the text boxes as you've done before.

Case 1

Based on what you learned in the text and using the Sample Company, you are to add the following activities to your company:

1   Open and review your previously customized report named Trial Balance 1/31/18.

2   Record the appropriate adjusting journal entries on 1/31/18 based on the following:

   a.   An inventory of supplies reveals that only $75 of supplies remain as of 1/31/18.

   b. $800 of prepaid expenses expired (representing prepaid rent) in the month of January.

   c.   A bill for $150 was received and recorded in the next month for repairs and maintenance consumed in the current month. Create a new liability account as you did earlier in the chapter.

   d.   Consulting services recorded on sales receipt #1004 for $2,500.00 to Surf Rider Foundation were never performed even though cash had been received. Thus, the revenue had not been earned. Create a new liability account as you did earlier in the chapter.

   e.   Consulting services of $8,500 were performed on the last day of the month for a new customer: Blazing Boards but not invoiced to the customer or recorded into the accounting records until a few days into the next month. Create a new asset account as you did earlier in the chapter.

   f.   Depreciation Expense of $575 ($75 and $500 for Equipment and Furniture & Fixtures, respectively) needed to be recorded for the month. Before recording this journal entry, edit the "Depreciation" expense account so that the new name is "Depreciation Expense." Also, change the account title for Furniture & Fixtures accumulated depreciation from "Depreciation" to "Accumulated Depreciation" as you did earlier in the chapter.

3   Open, print, and export to Excel your previously customized report named Trial Balance 1/31/18, which should now reflect your adjusting journal entries.

4   Open, print, and export to Excel your previously customized report named Transaction Detail by Account, which should now reflect your adjusting journal entries.

Case 2

Based on what you learned in the text and using the Sample Company, you are to add the following activities to your company:

1   Open and review your previously customized report named Trial Balance 1/31/19.

2 Record the appropriate adjusting journal entries on 1/31/19 based on the following:

   a. An inventory of supplies reveals that only $200 of supplies remain as of 1/31/19.

   b. $1,800 of prepaid expenses expired (representing prepaid insurance) in the month of January.

   c. A bill for $750 was received and recorded in the next month for legal fees performed in the current month. Create a new liability account as you did earlier in the chapter.

   d. Custom painting services recorded on invoice #1003 for $4,500.00 to Hagen's toys were never performed even though invoiced. Thus, the revenue had not been earned. Create a new liability account as you did earlier in the chapter.

   e. Repair services of $6,298 were performed on the last day of the month for a new customer: Kelly's Awesome Copters but not invoiced to the customer or recorded into the accounting records until a few days into the next month. Create a new asset account as you did earlier in the chapter.

   f. Depreciation Expense of $1,000 ($375 and $625 for Furniture and Machinery & Equipment, respectively) needed to be recorded for the month. Before recording this journal entry edit the "Depreciation" expense account so the new name is "Depreciation Expense." Also, change the account title for Machinery & Equipment accumulated depreciation from "Depreciation" to "Accumulated Depreciation" like you did in the chapter.

3 Open, print, and export to Excel your previously customized report named Trial Balance 1/31/19, which should reflect your adjusting journal entries.

4 Open, print, and export to Excel your previously customized report named Transaction Detail by Account, which should reflect your adjusting journal entries.

Case 3

Based on what you learned in the text, using the Sample Company, you are to add the following activities to your company:

1 Open and review your previously customized report named Trial Balance 1/31/20.

2 Record the appropriate adjusting journal entries on 1/31/20 based on the following:

   a. An inventory of supplies reveals that only $200 of supplies remain as of 1/31/20.

   b. $1,500 of prepaid expenses expired (representing prepaid insurance) in the month of January.

c. A bill for $350 was received and recorded in the next month from FixIt, Inc. for repairs performed in the current month. Create a new liability account like you did in the chapter.

d. Phone Consulting services recorded on invoice #1003 for $210.00 to Diamond Girl, Inc. were never performed even though invoiced. Thus, the revenue had not been earned. Create a new liability account like you did in the chapter.

e. Phone Consulting services of $1,800 were performed on the last day of the month for a new customer: Graham Engineering, Inc. but not invoiced to the customer or recorded into the accounting records until a few days into the next month. Create a new asset account like you did in the chapter.

f. Depreciation Expense of $1,200 ($850 and $350 for Buildings and Machinery & Equipment respectively) needed to be recorded for the month. Before recording this journal entry, edit the "Depreciation" expense account so that the new name is "Depreciation Expense." Also change the account title for the Machinery & Equipment accumulated depreciation account from "Depreciation" to "Accumulated Depreciation" like you did in the chapter.

3 Open, print, and export to Excel your previously customized report named Trial Balance 1/31/20, which should now reflect your adjusting journal entries.

4 Open, print, and export to Excel your previously customized report named Transaction Detail by Account, which should now reflect your adjusting journal entries.

Financial Statements and Reports

10

Student Learning Outcomes

Upon completion of this chapter, the student will be able to do the following:

- Create an income statement
- Create a balance sheet
- Create a statement of cash flows
- Create an accounts receivable aging summary
- Create an accounts payable aging summary
- Create an inventory valuation summary
- Customize and save reports

Overview

Intuit has provided a Sample Company online to let new users test drive its QBO product. In this chapter, you will open this Sample Company and practice creating reports in QBO. Prior to the creation of periodic financial statements, generally accepted accounting principles (GAAP) require that accounting records be adjusted to reflect accrual accounting. You completed that process in the previous chapter.

Four standard reports exist in financial accounting: the income statement, the statement of stockholders' equity, the balance sheet, and the statement of cash flows. QBO does not have a report for stockholders' equity. It does have the others along with a host of other reports so you can understand the underlying business events that have occurred during a particular accounting period. You will be exploring the A/R Aging Summary, A/P Aging Summary, and Inventory Valuation Summary reports. You will also be customizing them by adding columns, removing cents,

Remember, if you stop in the middle of this work, none of your work will be saved. So, when you return, the same Sample Company, without your work, will appear. In some parts of the chapter, you will be asked to sign out of the Sample Company and sign back in so the Sample Company is reset to its original state. In the end of chapter work, you will be asked to perform the same tasks completed on the Sample Company on your Student Company. That work, of course, will be saved.

Income Statement

In this section, you will create an income statement. Intuit decided years ago to call this report Profit and Loss rather than an Income Statement. Even though this may confuse the accounting professional and accounting student, it resonates with the small business user that uses QBO. This report is designed to communicate the revenues earned and expenses incurred for a business over a month, quarter, or year.

Intuit defines this report as follows: "Shows money you earned (income) and money you spent (expenses) so you can see how profitable you are." That is not exactly how an accounting professional or accounting student was taught but close enough. Accountants define the income statement as a report reflecting revenues less expenses to derive net income. Intuit is not about to change its wording to accommodate us, so we will accept it at face value. Thus, revenues are the same as income in the Profit and Loss report. For simplicity, we will refer to this as the Profit and Loss report.

To create a Profit and Loss report for the Sample Company, do the following:

1   Open your Internet browser.

2   Type **https://qbo.intuit.com/redir/testdrive** into your browser's address text box, and then press [**Enter**] to view the Sample Company Home page.

3   Click **Reports** from the navigation bar.

4   Type **Profit and Loss** in the Go to report search box and the press [**Enter**].

5   Click the **Collapse** button to provide a more summarized version to view the report shown in Figure 10.1.

Figure 10.1

Profit and Loss report (collapsed and partial views)

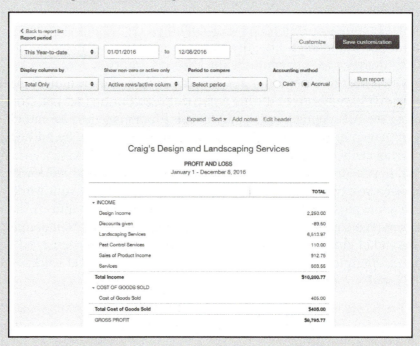

You recall that when using the Sample Company, dates change based upon the system date of Intuit's servers on which these data reside. The system date was 12/8/16 when this report was created; therefore, the default dates for this report were 1/1/16 to 12/8/16 as seen in the Report period text boxes at the top of Figure 10.1.

6 Change the From: date to the first of the previous month and the To: date to the last day of the previous month and click **Run Report**. Since the system date was 12/8/16 when this report was created, the report shown in Figure 10.2 is for the period 11/1/16 to 11/30/16. Your report will have a different period than that shown next.

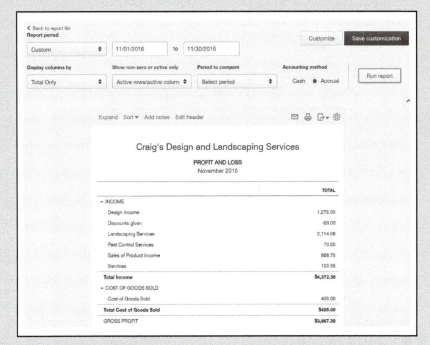

Figure 10.2

Profit and Loss Report (partial view)

Trouble? If you are doing this work in a different year, 2017, for example, you may have to type a different year and a different month to view the data.

By defining the accounting period as I did earlier for the month of November 2016, the only events reported are those recorded during that period. All reports in QBO allow you to drill down to specific transactions recorded in that period. You drill down by clicking an account on a report. That reveals a transactions report for that account for that period. Double clicking a specific transaction in the transactions report reveals a specific source document such as an invoice, sales receipt, cash receipt, bill, etc. Recall the Trouble? earlier. The amounts you are asked to investigate next will most likely be different than that stated in the steps. Remember you're just using the Sample Company to explore. You will not find these issues in the end-of-chapter case problems.

7 Click the **1,275.00** amount (or whatever amount is shown) next to the Design income account as shown in Figure 10.3 to view the Transaction report for the Design income account for the month of November shown in Figure 10.3, remembering that this figure illustrates the details behind the number you just clicked.

Figure 10.3

Transaction Report (for the design income account)

8 Click on the **Dylan Sollfrank** sales receipt to view Sales Receipt #1003 shown in Figure 10.4.

Figure 10.4

Sales Receipt #1003

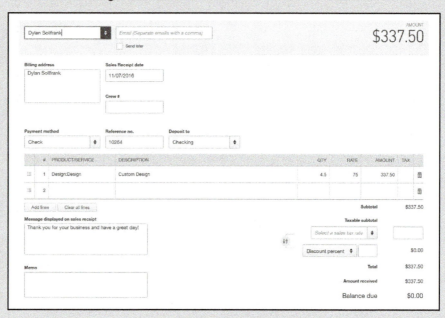

9 Click **Cancel** to return to the transaction report, and click **Back to report summary** to return to the Profit and Loss report.

Balance Sheet

In this section, you will create a balance sheet that reports on your company's assets, liabilities, and stockholders' equity as of a specific date (not period). However, when creating this report, QBO provides you the ability to define the period in which underlying account balances will reflect in their transactions reports. QBO default is this Year-to-date. Recall the **Trouble?** earlier. The amounts you are asked to investigate next will most likely be different than that stated in the steps. Remember you're just using the Sample Company to explore. You will not find these issues in the end-of-chapter case problems.

To create a balance sheet, do the following:

1 Continue from where you left off. If you closed the Sample Company, follow the steps to reopen it found at the beginning of this chapter.

2 Click **Reports** from the navigation bar.

3 Type **Balance Sheet** in the Go to report search box, and press [**Enter**] to view the partial balance sheet shown in Figure 10.5.

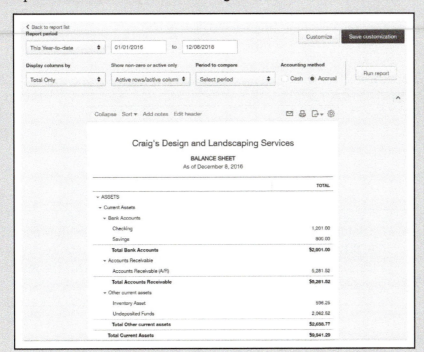

Figure 10.5

Balance Sheet (partial view)

4 The system date was 12/8/16 when this report was created (yours will be your current system date); therefore, the default dates for this report were 1/1/16 to 12/8/16 as seen in the Report period text boxes at the top of Figure 10.5. Change the From: date to the first of the previous month and the To: date to the last day of the previous month like you did previously with the profit and loss statement and click **Run Report**. Since the system date was 12/8/16 when this report was created, the report shown in Figure 10.6 is for the period 11/1/16 to 11/30/16. Your report will have a different period than that shown next.

Figure 10.6

Balance Sheet (partial view)

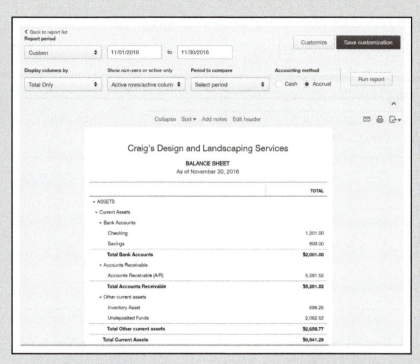

5 Click the Accounts Receivable (A/R) balance that, as shown in Figure 10.6, is **5,281.52** (or whatever balance is shown for Accounts Receivable) to view a transaction report for Accounts Receivable (A/R) for the month you specified shown in Figure 10.7. (Your balance may differ.)

Figure 10.7

Transaction Report (for Accounts Receivable (A/R): partial view)

Craig's Design and Landscaping Services

TRANSACTION REPORT
January 1 - December 8, 2016

DATE	TRANSACTION TYPE	NUM	NAME	MEMO/DESCRIPTION	ACCOUNT	SPLIT	AMOUNT	BALANCE
▾ Accounts Receivable (A/R)								
07/28/2016	Invoice	1002	Bill's Windsurf Shop		Accounts Receivable (A/R)	-Split-	175.00	175.00
07/28/2016	Invoice	1030	Freeman Sporting Goods:0969 ...		Accounts Receivable (A/R)	-Split-	226.75	401.75
08/18/2016	Payment	1053	Bill's Windsurf Shop		Accounts Receivable (A/R)	Checking	-175.00	226.75
08/19/2016	Payment		Freeman Sporting Goods:0969 ...		Accounts Receivable (A/R)	Undeposited Funds	-226.75	0.00
08/29/2016	Invoice	1031	Freeman Sporting Goods:0969 ...		Accounts Receivable (A/R)	-Split-	387.00	387.00
09/04/2016	Invoice	1024	Red Rock Diner		Accounts Receivable (A/R)	-Split-	156.00	543.00
09/24/2016	Invoice	1016	Kookies by Kathy		Accounts Receivable (A/R)	Landscaping Services	75.00	618.00
09/25/2016	Invoice	1028	Freeman Sporting Goods:55 Tw...		Accounts Receivable (A/R)	-Split-	81.00	699.00
09/25/2016	Invoice	1025	Amy's Bird Sanctuary		Accounts Receivable (A/R)	-Split-	205.00	904.00
09/25/2016	Invoice	1027	Bill's Windsurf Shop		Accounts Receivable (A/R)	-Split-	85.00	989.00
09/25/2016	Invoice	1029	Dukes Basketball Camp		Accounts Receivable (A/R)	-Split-	460.40	1,449.40

6 Scroll to the end of this report to view the ending balance of 5,281.52 (or whatever balance you have), which matches the Balance Sheet report shown in Figure 10.8.

Figure 10.8

Transaction Report end (for Accounts Receivable)

11/11/2016	Payment		Amy's Bird Sanctuary		Accounts Receivable (A/R)	Undeposited Funds	-220.00	6,190.19
11/12/2016	Invoice	1036	Freeman Sporting Goods:0969 ...		Accounts Receivable (A/R)	-Split-	477.50	6,667.69
11/12/2016	Invoice	1035	Mark Cho		Accounts Receivable (A/R)	-Split-	314.28	6,981.97
11/12/2016	Payment		Freeman Sporting Goods:0969 ...		Accounts Receivable (A/R)	Undeposited Funds	-387.00	6,594.97
11/12/2016	Payment		Cool Cars		Accounts Receivable (A/R)	Undeposited Funds	-1,675.52	4,919.45
11/12/2016	Invoice	1037	Sonnenschein Family Store		Accounts Receivable (A/R)	-Split-	362.07	5,281.52
Total for Accounts Receivable (A/R)							**$5,281.52**	
TOTAL							**$5,281.52**	

7 Click **−1.675.52**, which is the last transaction shown (a payment from Cool Cars) to view the receive payment window shown in Figure 10.9.

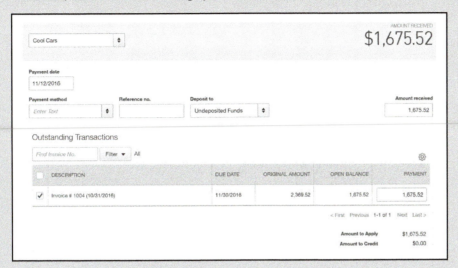

Figure 10.9

Payment Received (from Cool Cars)

8 Click **Cancel** to return to the transaction report, and click **Back to report summary** to return to the Balance Sheet.

Statement of Cash Flows

In this section, you will create a statement of cash flows, which reports on a company's operating, investing, and financing activities. Recall the Trouble? earlier. The amounts you are asked to investigate next will most likely be different than that stated in the steps. Remember you're just using the Sample Company to explore. You will not find these issues in the end-of-chapter case problems.

To create a statement of cash flows, do the following:

1 Continue from where you left off. If you closed the Sample Company, follow the steps to reopen it found at the beginning of this chapter.

2 Click **Reports** from the navigation bar.

3 Type **Statement of Cash Flows** in the Go to report search box, and press **[Enter]** to view the partial statement of cash flows shown in Figure 10.10.

Figure 10.10

Statement of Cash Flows
(partial view)

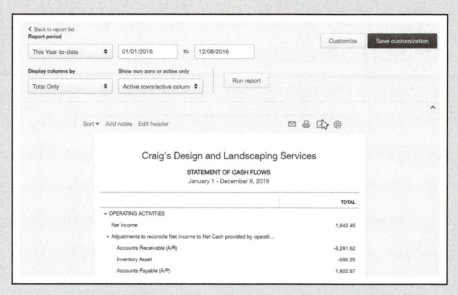

4   The system date was 12/8/16 when this report was created; therefore, the default dates for this report were 1/1/16 to 12/8/16 as seen in the Report period text boxes at the top of Figure 10.10. Change the From: date to the first of the previous month and the To: date to the last day of the previous month like you did previously with the balance sheet and click **Run Report**. Since the system date was 12/8/16 when this report was created, the report shown in Figure 10.11 is for the period 11/1/16 to 11/30/16. Your report will have a different period than that shown next.

Figure 10.11

Statement of Cash Flows
(partial view)

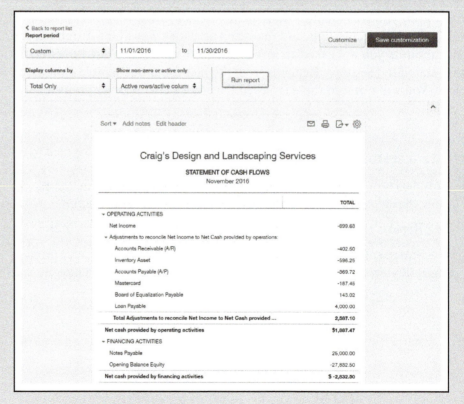

5 Click the Notes Payable balance that, as shown in Figure 10.11, is **25,000.00** to view a transaction report for Notes Payable for July shown in Figure 10.12. (Your balance may differ.)

Figure 10.12

Transaction Report (for notes payable)

6 Click **25,000.00** to view the journal entry shown in Figure 10.13.

Figure 10.13

Journal date (entry to record the notes payable opening balance)

7 Click **Cancel** to return to the transaction report, and click **Back to report summary** to return to the Statement of Cash Flows.

Accounts Receivable Aging Summary

In this section, you will create an accounts receivable aging summary, which reflects unpaid invoices for the current period and for the last 30, 60, and 90+ days as of a specific date. Aging summaries help find customers who may be delinquent in their payments and help a company estimate the need for an allowance for uncollectible accounts. Aging information must take into consideration the company's normal terms for a customer. For example, it would not be an issue if many customers are in the 60+ category, but the normal terms for those customers are net 60. However, it would be an issue if the normal terms are net 30 and the same situation existed. Recall the **Trouble?** earlier. The amounts you are asked to investigate next will most likely be different than that stated in the steps. Remember you're just using the Sample Company to explore. You will not find these issues in the end-of-chapter case problems.

To create an accounts receivable aging summary report, do the following:

1   Continue from where you left off. If you closed the Sample Company, follow the steps to reopen it found at the beginning of this chapter.

2   Click **Reports** from the navigation bar.

3   Type **A/R Aging Summary** in the Go to report search box, and press [**Enter**] to view the accounts receivable (A/R) aging report. Change the "as of" date to the end of the month prior to your system date. In this case, since the system date was 12/8/16, the "as of" date was changed to 11/30/16 then click **Run Report** to view the report shown in Figure 10.14.

Figure 10.14

Accounts Receivable (A/R) Aging Summary

Craig's Design and Landscaping Services

A/R AGING SUMMARY
As of November 30, 2016

	CURRENT	1 - 30	31 - 60	61 - 90	91 AND OVER	TOTAL
Amy's Bird Sanctuary		239.00				$239.00
Bill's Windsurf Shop			85.00			$85.00
▼ Freeman Sporting Goods						$0.00
0969 Ocean View Road	477.50					$477.50
55 Twin Lane	4.00		81.00			$85.00
Total Freeman Sporting Goods	**481.50**		**81.00**			**$562.50**
Geeta Kalapatapu	629.10					$629.10
Jeff's Jalopies		81.00				$81.00
John Melton		450.00				$450.00
Kookies by Kathy			75.00			$75.00
Mark Cho	314.28					$314.28
Paulsen Medical Supplies	954.75					$954.75
Red Rock Diner	70.00		156.00			$226.00
Rondonuwu Fruit and Vegi	78.60					$78.60
▼ Shara Barnett						$0.00
Barnett Design		274.50				$274.50
Total Shara Barnett		**274.50**				**$274.50**
Sonnenschein Family Store	362.07					$362.07
Sushi by Katsuyuki	160.00					$160.00
Travis Waldron	414.72					$414.72
Weiskopf Consulting	375.00					$375.00
TOTAL	**$3,840.02**	**$1,044.50**	**$397.00**	**$0.00**	**$0.00**	**$5,281.52**

4   Click on the **85.00** owed by Bill's Windsurf Shop shown in Figure 10.14 to view A/R Aging Detail report shown in Figure 10.15.

Figure 10.15

Accounts Receivable (A/R) Aging Detail Report

Craig's Design and Landscaping Services

A/R AGING DETAIL
As of November 30, 2016

DATE	TRANSACTION TYPE	NUM	CUSTOMER	DUE DATE	AMOUNT	OPEN BALANCE
▼ 31 - 60 days past due						
09/25/2016	Invoice	1027	Bill's Windsurf Shop	10/25/2016	85.00	85.00
Total for 31 - 60 days past due					$85.00	$85.00
TOTAL					$85.00	$85.00

5 Click **85.00** to view invoice #1027 shown in Figure 10.16.

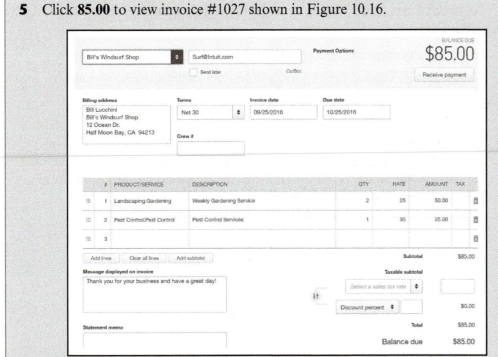

Figure 10.16

Invoice #1027 (to Bill's Windsurf Shop)

6 Call Bill to find out when he is planning to pay you. Actually, no, do not do that. Instead, click **Cancel** to return to the detail report, and click **Back to report summary** to return to the A/R Aging Summary report.

Accounts Payable Aging Summary

In this section, you will create an accounts payable aging summary, which reflects unpaid bills for the current period and for the last 30, 60, and 90+ days as of a specific date. Aging summaries help prioritize the payment of bills. Aging information must take into consideration the company's normal terms from a vendor. For example, it would not be an issue if a large amount of vendors bills are in the 60+ category, but the normal terms for those vendors are net 60. However, it would be an issue if the normal terms are net 30, and the same situation existed. Recall the **Trouble?** earlier. The amounts you are asked to investigate next will most likely be different than that stated in the steps. Remember you're just using the Sample Company to explore. You will not find these issues in the end-of-chapter case problems.

To create an accounts payable aging summary report, do the following:

1 Continue from where you left off. If you closed the Sample Company, follow the steps to reopen it found at the beginning of this chapter.

2 Click **Reports** from the navigation bar.

3 Type **A/P Aging Summary** in the Go to report search box, and press **[Enter]** to view the accounts payable aging report. Change the "as of" date to the end of the month prior to your system date. In this case, since the system date was 12/8/16, the "as of" date was changed to 11/30/16 then click **Run Report** to view the report shown in Figure 10.17.

Figure 10.17

Accounts Payable (A/P) Aging Summary

Craig's Design and Landscaping Services

A/P AGING SUMMARY
As of November 30, 2016

	CURRENT	1 - 30	31 - 60	61 - 90	91 AND OVER	TOTAL
Brosnahan Insurance Agency		241.23				$241.23
Diego's Road Warrior Bodyshop	755.00					$755.00
Norton Lumber and Building Mat...		205.00				$205.00
PG&E			86.44			$86.44
Robertson & Associates		315.00				$315.00
TOTAL	$755.00	$761.23	$86.44	$0.00	$0.00	$1,602.67

4 Click on the **86.44** owed to PG&E shown in Figure 10.17 to view A/P Aging Detail report shown in Figure 10.18.

Figure 10.18

Accounts Payable (A/P) Aging Detail Report

Craig's Design and Landscaping Services

A/P AGING DETAIL
As of November 30, 2016

DATE	TRANSACTION TYPE	NUM	VENDOR	DUE DATE	PAST DUE	AMOUNT	OPEN BALANCE
▾ 31 - 60 days past due							
09/28/2016	Bill		PG&E	10/28/2016	41	86.44	86.44
Total for 31 - 60 days past due						$86.44	$86.44
TOTAL						$86.44	$86.44

5 Click **86.44** to view the bill shown in Figure 10.19.

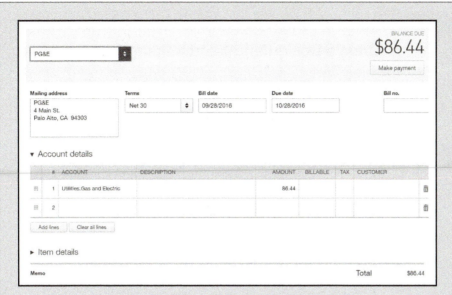

Figure 10.19

Bill (from PG&E)

6 Write a check to PG&E before the power gets cut off. Actually, no, do not do that. Instead, click **Cancel** to return to the detail report, and click **Back to report summary** to return to the A/P Aging Summary report.

Inventory Valuation Summary

In this section, you will create an inventory valuation summary that reflects each inventory item's quantity on hand, its average cost, and the resulting valuation as of a specific date. Recall the **Trouble?** earlier. The amounts you are asked to investigate next will most likely be different than that stated in the steps. Remember you're just using the Sample Company to explore. You will not find these issues in the end-of-chapter case problems.

To create an inventory valuation summary report, do the following:

1 Continue from where you left off. If you closed the Sample Company, follow the steps to reopen it found at the beginning of this chapter.

2 Click **Reports** from the navigation bar.

3 Type **Inventory Valuation Summary** in the Go to report search box, and press [**Enter**] to view the inventory valuation summary report. Change the "as of" date to the end of the month prior to your system date. In this case, since the system date was 12/8/16, the "as of" date was changed to 11/30/16 then click **Run Report** to view the report shown in Figure 10.20.

Figure 10.20

Inventory Valuation Summary

Craig's Design and Landscaping Services

INVENTORY VALUATION SUMMARY
As of November 30, 2016

	SKU	QTY	ASSET VALUE	AVG COST
▾ Design				
▾ Fountains				
Pump	P461-17	25.00	250.00	10.00
Rock Fountain	R154-88	2.00	250.00	125.00
Total Fountains			**500.00**	
Total Design			**500.00**	
▾ Landscaping				
▾ Sprinklers				
Sprinkler Heads	S867-56	25.00	18.75	0.75
Sprinkler Pipes	S867-62	31.00	77.50	2.50
Total Sprinklers			**96.25**	
Total Landscaping			**96.25**	
TOTAL			**$596.25**	

4 Click on the **25** representing the number of pumps on hand shown in Figure 10.20 to view an Inventory Valuation Detail report shown in Figure 10.21.

Figure 10.21

Inventory Valuation Detail

Craig's Design and Landscaping Services

INVENTORY VALUATION DETAIL
As of November 30, 2016

DATE	TRANSACTION TYPE	NUM	QTY	RATE	FIFO COST	QTY ON HAND	ASSET VALUE
▾ Design							
▾ Fountains							
▾ Pump							
11/12/2016	Inventory Qty Adjust	START	16.00	10.00	160.00	16.00	160.00
11/12/2016	Check	75	3.00	10.00	30.00	19.00	190.00
11/12/2016	Bill		8.00	10.00	80.00	27.00	270.00
11/12/2016	Invoice	1036	-1.00	10.00	-10.00	26.00	260.00
11/12/2016	Invoice	1037	-1.00	10.00	-10.00	25.00	250.00
Total for Pump			**25.00**		**$250.00**	**25.00**	**$250.00**
Total for Fountains			**25.00**		**$250.00**	**25.00**	**$250.00**
Total for Design			**25.00**		**$250.00**	**25.00**	**$250.00**

5 Click **Bill** reflecting the purchase of eight pumps shown in Figure 10.21 to view the bill shown in Figure 10.22.

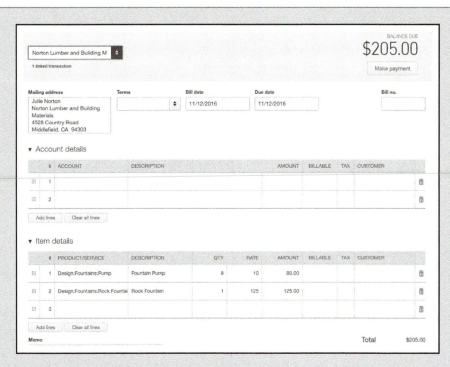

Figure 10.22

Bill (from Norton Lumber for the purchase of eight pumps)

6 Click **Cancel** to return to the detail report, and click **Back to report summary** to return to the A/P Aging Summary report.

Customizing and Saving Reports

All of the reports available in QBO can be customized in some fashion and saved for later use. In this section, you will customize a Profit and Loss report as an example. Recall the **Trouble?** earlier. The amounts you are asked to investigate next will most likely be different than that stated in the steps. Remember you're just using the Sample Company to explore. You will not find these issues in the end-of-chapter case problems.

To customize and save a Profit and Loss report, do the following:

1 Continue from where you left off. If you closed the Sample Company, follow the steps to reopen it found at the beginning of this chapter.

2 Click **Reports** from the navigation bar.

3 Type **Profit and Loss** in the Go to report search box and press [**Enter**].

4 Click **Collapse**.

5 Type **6/1/16** in the From: date text box and **7/31/16** in the To: date text box, and click **Run Report** to view the Profit and Loss report. Change the From: date to the first of the month 3 months prior to your system date and the To: date to the end of the month prior to your system date. In this case, since the system date was 12/8/16, the From: date was changed to 9/1/16 and the To: date was changed to 11/30/16. Then click **Run Report** to view the report shown in Figure 10.23.

Figure 10.23

Profit and Loss report
(for a three month period)

Craig's Design and Landscaping Services

PROFIT AND LOSS
September - November, 2016

	TOTAL
▾ INCOME	
Design income	2,250.00
Discounts given	-89.50
Landscaping Services	5,827.72
Pest Control Services	40.00
Sales of Product Income	912.75
Services	503.55
Total Income	**$9,444.52**
▾ COST OF GOODS SOLD	
Cost of Goods Sold	405.00
Total Cost of Goods Sold	**$405.00**
GROSS PROFIT	**$9,039.52**
▾ EXPENSES	
Advertising	74.86
Automobile	429.37
Equipment Rental	112.00
Insurance	241.23
Job Expenses	957.89
Legal & Professional Fees	670.00
Maintenance and Repair	940.00
Meals and Entertainment	28.49
Office Expenses	18.08
Rent or Lease	900.00
Utilities	331.39
Total Expenses	**$4,903.31**
NET OPERATING INCOME	**$4,136.21**
▾ OTHER EXPENSES	
Miscellaneous	2,916.00
Total Other Expenses	**$2,916.00**
NET OTHER INCOME	$ -2,916.00
NET INCOME	$1,220.21

6 Click **Customize**, click Rows/Columns, and then select **Months** from the Columns drop-down list in the Rows/Columns section of the Customize Profit and Loss window shown in Figure 10.24.

Figure 10.24

Customize Profit and Loss report

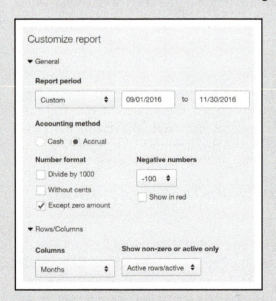

7 Scroll down the Customize Profit and Loss window, and place a check in the **% of Income** check box.

8 Click **Run Report** to view the customized Profit and Loss report shown in Figure 10.25.

Figure 10.25

Profit and Loss report (customized version)

Craig's Design and Landscaping Services

PROFIT AND LOSS

September - November, 2016

	SEP 2016		OCT 2016		NOV 2016		TOTAL	
	CURRENT	% OF INCOME	CURRENT	% OF INCOME	CURRENT	% OF INCOME	CURRENT	% OF INCOME
INCOME								
Design income			975.00	24.05 %	1,275.00	29.16 %	$2,250.00	23.82 %
Discounts given			-30.50	-0.75 %	-59.00	-1.35 %	$ -89.50	-0.95 %
Landscaping Services	948.00	93.12 %	2,765.64	68.22 %	2,114.08	48.35 %	$5,827.72	61.70 %
Pest Control Services	70.00	6.88 %	-100.00	-2.47 %	70.00	1.60 %	$40.00	0.42 %
Sales of Product Income			44.00	1.09 %	868.75	19.87 %	$912.75	9.66 %
Services			400.00	9.87 %	103.55	2.37 %	$503.55	5.33 %
Total Income	**$1,018.00**	**100.00 %**	**$4,054.14**	**100.00 %**	**$4,372.38**	**100.00 %**	**$9,444.52**	**100.00 %**
COST OF GOODS SOLD								
Cost of Goods Sold					405.00	9.26 %	$405.00	4.29 %
Total Cost of Goods Sold	**$0.00**	**0.00%**	**$0.00**	**0.00%**	**$405.00**	**9.26 %**	**$405.00**	**4.29 %**
GROSS PROFIT	**$1,018.00**	**100.00 %**	**$4,054.14**	**100.00 %**	**$3,967.38**	**90.74 %**	**$9,039.52**	**95.71 %**
EXPENSES								
Advertising					74.86	1.71 %	$74.86	0.79 %
Automobile	54.55	5.36 %	127.01	3.13 %	247.81	5.67 %	$429.37	4.55 %
Equipment Rental					112.00	2.56 %	$112.00	1.19 %
Insurance					241.23	5.52 %	$241.23	2.55 %
Job Expenses	158.08	15.53 %	285.27	7.04 %	514.54	11.77 %	$957.89	10.14 %
Legal & Professional Fees	250.00	24.56 %	130.00	3.21 %	490.00	11.21 %	$870.00	9.21 %
Maintenance and Repair					940.00	21.50 %	$940.00	9.95 %
Meals and Entertainment					28.49	0.65 %	$28.49	0.30 %
Office Expenses					18.08	0.41 %	$18.08	0.19 %
Rent or Lease			900.00	22.20 %			$900.00	9.53 %
Utilities	142.94	14.04 %	188.45	4.65 %			$331.39	3.51 %
Total Expenses	**$605.57**	**59.49 %**	**$1,630.73**	**40.22 %**	**$2,867.01**	**61.00 %**	**$4,903.31**	**51.92 %**
NET OPERATING INCOME	**$412.43**	**40.51 %**	**$2,423.41**	**59.78 %**	**$1,300.37**	**29.74 %**	**$4,136.21**	**43.79 %**
OTHER EXPENSES								
Miscellaneous			916.00	22.59 %	2,000.00	45.74 %	$2,916.00	30.88 %
Total Other Expenses	**$0.00**	**0.00%**	**$916.00**	**22.59 %**	**$2,000.00**	**45.74 %**	**$2,916.00**	**30.88 %**
NET OTHER INCOME	**$0.00**	**0.00 %**	**$ -916.00**	**-22.59 %**	**$ -2,000.00**	**-45.74 %**	**$ -2,916.00**	**-30.88 %**
NET INCOME	**$412.43**	**40.51 %**	**$1,507.41**	**37.18 %**	**$ -699.63**	**-16.00 %**	**$1,220.21**	**12.92 %**

9 Click **Save Customizations**.

10 Type **Profit and Loss Comparison** as the new name for this report, and share it as you have done in the previous chapters.

End Note

In this chapter, you did not add business events, but you did create the basic financial statement reports: profit and loss, balance sheet, and statement of cash flows. In addition, you drilled down beyond those reports to transaction detail reports and to source documents like payments, invoices, bills, etc. You created some analytical reports to learn more about accounts receivable, accounts payable, and inventory. Lastly, you learned how to customize reports and save those reports for later use.

Chapter 10 Questions

View the sample company QBO file to answer these questions by creating reports:

1   Invoice 1015 was created for which customer?

2   What was the first item sold on invoice 1015?

3   What was the last item sold that was categorized as sales of product income?

4   Who sent a bill for $315.00 in accounting fees?

5   How many sprinkler head are currently on hand?

6   What is the average cost per unit of sprinkler heads?

7   Who is the most delinquent customer?

8   What is the total amount of receivables that are current?

9   What amount of payables are 1–30 days past due?

10 What amount of cash was provided by financing activities?

Chapter 10 Matching

a. Income statement

b. Balance sheet

c. Statement of cash flows

d. AR aging report

e. AP aging report

f. Inventory valuation report

g. Profit and loss report

h. To view a transaction report

i. To view a source document

j. % of income check box

_____ Click on an event in any transaction report

_____ Click an account on any report

_____ Click to add a new column in a report

_____ Reflects unpaid bills for the current period

_____ Reports revenues and expenses

_____ Includes operating, investing, and financing activities

_____ Reports inventory quantities on hand

_____ Reports assets, liabilities, and equities

_____ Another name for the income statement

_____ Reflects unpaid invoices for the current period

Chapter 10 Cases

The following cases require you to open the company you updated in Chapter 9. Each of the following cases continues throughout the text in a sequential manner. Each of the following cases is similar in concepts assessed but differ in amounts and transactions.

To reopen your company, do the following:

1 Open your Internet browser.

2 Type **https://qbo.intuit.com/qbo28/login?webredir** into your browser's address text box.

3 Type your User ID and Password into the text boxes as you have earlier.

Case 1

Based on what you learned in the chapter and using the Sample Company, you are to create the following reports for your company continuing from Chapter 9:

1 Create, print, and export to Excel a Profit and Loss report for January 2018. Customize this report by adding a percent of income column and saving and by sharing your customization as Profit and Loss Jan 2018.

2 Using the Profit and Loss report created above, drill down to a Transactions Report for the Sales account. Print and export this report to Excel. Save and share this report as a Sales Transaction Report.

3 Create, print, and export to Excel a Balance Sheet report as of 1/31/18. Customize this report by adding a percent of column and saving and sharing your customization as Balance Sheet Jan 2018.

4 Using the Balance Sheet report created above, drill down to a Transactions Report for the Checking account. Print and export this report to Excel. Save and share this report as Checking Report.

5 Create, print, and export to Excel a Statement of Cash Flows report as of 1/31/18. Save and share your customization as Statement of Cash Flows Jan 2018.

6 Using the Statement of Cash Flows report created above, drill down to a Transactions Report for the Accounts Receivable account. Print and export this report to Excel. Save and share this report as an A/R SCF Report.

7 Create, print, and export to Excel an A/R Aging Summary report for the month of January 2018. Save and share your customization as A/R Aging Summary Jan 2018.

8 Create, print, and export to Excel an A/P Aging Summary report for the month of January 2018. Save and share your customization as A/P Aging Summary Jan 2018.

9 Create, print, and export to Excel an Inventory Valuation Summary report for the month of January 2018. Save and share your customization as an Inventory Valuation Summary Jan 2018.

Case 2

Based on what you learned in the chapter and using the Sample Company, you are to create the following reports for your company continuing from Chapter 9:

1 Create, print, and export to Excel a Profit and Loss report for January 2019. Customize this report by adding a percent of income column. Save and share your customization as Profit and Loss Jan 2019.

2 Using the Profit and Loss report created above, drill down to a Transactions Report for the Insurance account. Print and export this report to Excel. Save and share this report as an Insurance Transaction Report.

3 Create, print, and export to Excel a Balance Sheet report as of 1/31/19. Customize this report by adding a percent of column. Save and share your customization as Balance Sheet Jan 2019.

4 Using the Balance Sheet report created above, drill down to a Transactions Report for the Inventory Asset account. Print and export this report to Excel. Save and share this report as Inventory Report.

5 Create, print, and export to Excel a Statement of Cash Flows report as of 1/31/19. Save and share your customization as Statement of Cash Flows Jan 2019.

6 Using the Statement of Cash Flows report created above, drill down to a Transactions Report for the Prepaid Expenses account. Print and export this report to Excel. Save and share this report as PPE SCF Report.

7 Create, print, and export to Excel an A/R Aging Summary report for the month of January 2019. Save and share your customization as an A/R Aging Summary Jan 2019.

8 Create, print, and export to Excel an A/P Aging Summary report for the month of January 2019. Save and share your customization as an A/P Aging Summary Jan 2019.

9 Create, print, and export to Excel an Inventory Valuation Summary report for January 2018. Save and share your customization as Inventory Valuation Summary Jan 2018.

Case 3

Based on what you learned in the chapter, using the Sample Company, you are to create the following reports for your company continuing from Chapter 9:

1 Create, print, and export to Excel a Profit and Loss report for the month of January 2020. Customize this report by adding a percent of income column and saving and sharing your customization as Profit and Loss Jan 2020.

2 Using the Profit and Loss report created earlier, drill down to a Transactions Report for the Advertising account. Print and export this report to Excel. Save and share this report as Advertising Transaction Report.

3 Create, print, and export to Excel a Balance Sheet report as of 1/31/20. Customize this report by adding a percent of row column and saving and sharing your customization as Balance Sheet Jan 2020.

4 Using the Balance Sheet report created earlier, drill down to a Transactions Report for the Accounts Receivable (A/R) account. Print and export this report to Excel. Save and share this report as AR Report.

5 Create, print, and export to Excel a Statement of Cash Flows report as of 1/31/20. Save and share your customization as Statement of Cash Flows Jan 2020.

6 Using the Statement of Cash Flows report created earlier, drill down to a Transactions Report for the Payroll Tax Payable account. Print and export this report to Excel. Save and share this report as Payroll Tax SCF Report.

7 Create, print, and export to Excel an A/R Aging Summary report for the month of January 2020. Save and share your customization as A/R Aging Summary Jan 2020.

8 Create, print, and export to Excel an A/P Aging Summary report for the month of January 2020. Save and share your customization as A/P Aging Summary Jan 2020.

9 Create, print, and export to Excel an Inventory Valuation Summary report for the month of January 2020. Save and share your customization as Inventory Valuation Summary Jan 2020.

1

Sales Tax

Some companies are required to collect sales tax from customers depending on the state(s) in which they do business. The following are steps necessary to set up a simplified sales tax.

To set up a company's sales tax:

1 Click **Sales Tax** from the navigation bar.

2 Click the **Set Up Sales Tax Rates** button to view the window shown in Figure A.1.

Figure A.1

Sales Tax Center

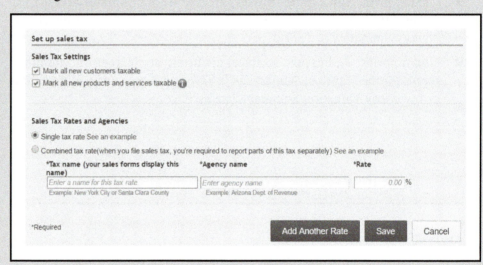

3 Type **California** in the Tax name text box.

4 Type **State Board of Equalization** in the Agency name text box.

5 Type **10** in the Rate text box. Your window should now look like Figure A.2.

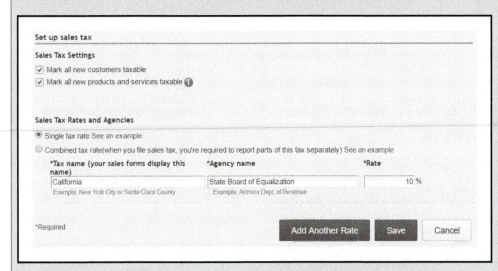

Figure A.2

Modified Sales Tax Center

6 Click **Save**.

Index

account(s). *See also* chart of accounts
   Accounts Payable
      establishing beginning balance, 41–42
      journalizing, 41–42
   Accounts Receivable
      establishing beginning balance, 41–42
      journalizing, 41–42
      reports, 30
   creating, 3–4
   Inventory Asset, 91
   Opening Balance Equity, 43–45
   Payroll (expense), 120
   Payroll Tax Payable (liability), 120
Account Quickreport, 27
Accounts Payable (A/P) account
   establishing beginning balance, 41–42
   journalizing, 41–42
   Transaction Report, 91
Accounts Payable (A/P) Aging Detail
   Report, 182
Accounts Payable (A/P) Aging Summary
   report, 181–183
Accounts Payable (A/P) Register page, 26
Accounts Receivable (A/R) account
   establishing beginning balance, 41–42
   journalizing, 41–42
   reports, 30
   Transaction reports, 176
Accounts Receivable (A/R) Aging Detail
   Report, 180
Accounts Receivable (A/R) Aging
   Summary reports, 179–181
accrued expenses, 161–162
accruing revenue, 163–164
Adding Inventory page, 39
adjusting entries, 156–166
   accrued expenses, 161–162
   accruing revenue, 163–164
   creating trial balance, 157
   depreciation, 164–166
   prepaid expenses
      deferring supplies as asset, 158
      recording consumption of supplies, 159–161
   types of, 156
   unearned revenue, 162–163
Advanced settings, 32
aging summaries
   Accounts Payable Aging Summary
      report, 181–183

Accounts Receivable Aging Summary
   reports, 179–181
A/P account. *See* Accounts Payable (A/P)
   account
A/P (Accounts Payable) Aging Detail
   Report, 182
A/P (Accounts Payable) Aging Summary
   report, 181–183
A/P (Accounts Payable) Register
   page, 26
A/R account. *See* Accounts Receivable
   (A/R) account
A/R (Accounts Receivable) Aging Detail
   Report, 180
A/R (Accounts Receivable) Aging
   Summary reports, 179–181

balance sheet, creating, 43–45, 175–177
Balance Sheet page, 44
Balance Sheet reports, 29
Bank and Credit Cards page, 22
bank deposit, inputting, 68
banking transactions, viewing, 21–23
bank reconciliations, 144–148
   creating, 145–148
   overview, 144–145
   Summary Reconciliation reports,
      147–148
Basic Info window, 5
bill(s). *See also* invoices
   adding purchase order information,
      84
   after adding purchase order information, 84–85
   credit card, 88–89
   entering, 83
   paying, 86–88
   for prepaid expenses, 86
   for services, 85–86
   from vendors for receipt of products
      or services, 83–86
budget(s)
   creating, 137–140
   reports related to, 140–144
      Budget Overview reports,
         141–142
      Budget *vs.* Actual reports,
         143–144
Budgeting window, 138
Budget Overview reports, 141–42
Budget *vs.* Actual reports, 143–144
Business Overview reports, 28

Case studies
   adjusting entries, 167–170
   budgets and bank reconciliations,
      149–155
   financial statements and reports,
      188–191
   investing and financing activities,
      111–117
   operating activities, purchases and
      cash payments, 94–101
   operating activities, sales and cash
      receipts, 71–77
   payroll, 128–136
   setting up company, 49–57
cash receipts, 65–68
chart of accounts. *See also* account(s)
   modifying, 37–42
      adding additional accounts,
         40–41
      adding checking accounts,
         37–38
      adding products and services,
         38–40
   viewing, 25–27
check payments, 89
common stock
   definition of, 106
   recording deposit of funds from sale
      of, 106–107
companies
   closing Opening Balance Equity
      account, 43–45
   establishing beginning balances, 36–42
   modifying chart of accounts, 36–42
   setting for, 35–36
   Transaction Detail by Account
      reports
Company Info window, 5–6
Company settings, 31
Create (+) menu, 8
Create window, 62, 64, 66, 68, 80
Credit Card Charge, 89
credit card payment, 88–89
customer
   accessing information about, 17–18
   adding, 61–62
Customer Information window, 61
Customers window, 8

deferring, definition of, 156
Deposit window, 68
depreciation, 102–103, 164–166

dividends
    definition of, 106
    payment of, 107

employees
    accessing information about, 20–21
    adding, 118–119
    paying, 121–127
        recording payment, 121–127
        recurring transactions, 124
        semi-monthly payroll information, 121, 125
Employees window, 9
Expenses settings, 32
expense transactions, viewing, 23–25
Expense window, 25

financial statements
    balance sheet, 175–177
    income statements
        creating, 172–174
        definition of, 172
        Profit and Loss Report, 172–173
        Sales Receipt, 174
        Transaction Report, 173–174
    Statement of Cash Flows, 177–179
financing activities. *See* investing and
    financing activities
fixed assets
    acquisition of in exchange for long-
        term debt, 109–110
    adding, 104
    definition of, 103
    depreciation, 102–103
    recording purchase of, 103–104

Gear window, 9–10

Help feature
    accessing, 11–13
    built-in resources, 11–13
    QuickBooks Community, 11–13
Help window, 12–13
Home page, 6–9

income statements, 172–174
    creating, 172–174
    definition of, 172
    Profit and Loss Report, 172–173
    Sales Receipt, 174
    Transaction Report, 173–174
Inventory Asset Account, 91
Inventory Valuation Detail, 184
Inventory Valuation Summary report,
    183–185
investing and financing activities
    acquisition of fixed assets in exchange
        for long-term debt, 109–110
    common stock and dividends,
        106–107

fixed assets, 102–104
long-term debt, 107–110
long-term investments, 105
invoices
    Accounts Receivable Aging Summary,
        181
    adding, 64–65
    sales, 62–65

journalizing
    Accounts Payable (A/P) account,
        41–42
    Accounts Receivable (A/R) account,
        41–42

lists
    of products and services, 59
    in QBO, 27–28
    viewing
        list of lists, 27
        list of terms, 28
long-term debt
    acquisition of fixed assets in exchange
        for, 109–110
    recording receipt of funds from bor-
        rowing, 108–109
    repayment with interest, 109
long-term investments
    definition of, 105
    recording purchase of, 105

Manage Users window, 10

Opening Balance Equity account, 43–45
operating activities
    purchases and cash payments, 78–92
        adding vendors, 78–79
        paying bills, 86–88
        purchase orders, 79–82
        recording bills, 83–86
        recording check payments, 89
        recording credit card payments,
            88–89
        trial balance, 90–92
    sales and cash receipts
        adding services, products, and
            customers, 58–62
        recording cash receipts, 65–68
        sales invoices, 62–65
        sales receipts, 62–65
        Transaction Detail by Account
            reports, 68–69

payments
    check, 89
    credit card, 88–89
    receipts of, 65–68
    recording, 121–127
payroll
    adding employees, 118–119

adding payroll-related accounts,
    120–121
paying employees, 121–127
    recording payments, 121–127
    recurring transactions, 124
    semi-monthly payroll informa-
        tion, 121, 125
    Transaction Report, 123, 126
    Trial Balance, 123, 126
Payroll (expense) account, 120
Payroll Tax Payable (liability) account, 120
prepaid expenses
    bills for, 86
    deferring supplies as asset, 158
    recording consumption of supplies,
        159–161
products
    adding, 60–61, 79–82
    lists of, 59
    Purchase Order, 80
    recording bills from vendors for
        receipt of, 83–86
Profit and Loss budget, 137–140
Profit and Loss report, 29. *See also* income
    statements
    creating, 172–173
    customizing, 185–187
    saving, 185–187
Purchase of Equipment, 104
Purchase Order, 80
purchases and cash payments, 78–92
    adding vendors, 78–79
    paying bills, 86–88
    purchase orders, 79–82
    recording bills, 83–86
    recording check payments, 89
    recording credit card payments, 88–89
    trial balance, 90–92

QuickBooks Accountant (QBDT), 2
QuickBooks Online Plus (QBO)
    assigning instructor as company
        "accountant", 10–11
    creating accounts, 3–4
    customization, 6
    definition of, 1
    versus desktop version of Quick-
        Books, 2–3
    Help feature, 11–13
    navigating within, 6–9
    providing user information, 4–6

receipts of payment (cash receipts), 65–68.
    See also sales and cash receipts
Receive Payment window, 66
Reconcile - Checking form, 146–147
Reconcile window, 145
reconciliation process, 145
recurring transactions, 124
report(s)

Accounts Payable Aging Detail, 182
Accounts Payable Aging Summary,
    181–183
accounts receivable, 30
Accounts Receivable Aging Detail
    Report, 180
Accounts Receivable Aging Summary,
    179–181
Balance Sheet, 29
Business Overview, 28
Inventory Valuation Summary,
    183–185
Profit and Loss, 172–173
Profit and Loss report, 29
Statement of Cash Flows, 30
Transaction
    for Accounts Payable account, 91
    for Accounts Receivable (A/R),
        176
    for checking account, 91
    income statements, 173–174
    for Inventory Asset Account, 91
    for supplies asset, 161
Transaction Detail by Account
    creating, 45–46, 68–69
    exporting, 45–46, 68–69
    printing, 45–46, 68–69
revenue
    accruing, 163–164
    unearned, 162–163

sales and cash receipts, 58–69
    adding services, products, and
        customers, 58–62
    recording cash receipts, 65–68
    sales invoices, 62–65
    sales receipts
        adding, 62–65
        definition of, 62
    Transaction Detail by Account
        reports, 68–69

Sales Receipt after Sales Tax, 63
Sales Receipt before Sales Tax, 63
sales receipts
    adding, 62–63
    income statements, 174
Sales settings, 31
sales transactions, viewing, 23–25
Sample Company
    accessing customer information,
        17–18
    accessing employee information,
        20–21
    accessing vendor information,
        18–20
    adding customers, 61–62
    adding new services, 58–60
    adding products, 60–61
    adding sales invoices, 62–65
    banking transactions, viewing,
        21–23
    cash receipts, 65–68
    chart of accounts, viewing, 25–27
    expense transactions, viewing, 23–25
    list of lists, viewing, 27
    list of terms, viewing, 28
    receipts of payment, 65–68
    sales transactions, viewing, 23–25
    settings management
        Advanced settings, 32
        Company settings, 31
        Expenses settings, 32
        Sales settings, 31
Sample Company Home page, 16
semi-monthly payroll information, 121,
    125
services
    adding, 58–60
    lists of, 59
    paying bills for, 85–86
    recording bills from vendors for
        receipt of, 83–86

settings management
    Advanced settings, 32
    Company settings, 31
    Expenses settings, 32
    Sales settings, 31
Set Up Your Account window, 3–4
Sign In Window, 49
Statement of Cash Flows, 30, 177–179
Summary Reconciliation reports,
    147–148

Transaction Detail by Account reports
    creating, 45–46, 68–69
    exporting, 45–46, 68–69
    printing, 45–46, 68–69
Transaction reports
    for Accounts Payable account, 91
    for Accounts Receivable (A/R), 176
    for checking account, 91
    income statements, 173–174
    for Inventory Asset Account, 91
    for notes payable, 179
    for supplies asset, 161
trial balance
    creating, 90–92, 157
    investigating, 90–92

unearned revenue, 162–163
user information, 4–6
Users window, 10

Vendor Information window, 78–79
vendors
    accessing information about, 18–20
    adding, 78–79
    recording bills for receipt of products
        or services, 83–86
Vendors window, 6, 9

Welcome Guide, 6–7